NORTHERN APPALACHIA REVIEW

VOLUME 2

CATAMOUNT
PRESS
an imprint of Sunbury Press, Inc.
Mechanicsburg, PA USA

an imprint of Sunbury Press, Inc.
Mechanicsburg, PA USA

For information about special discounts for bulk purchases, please contact Sunbury Press Orders Dept. at (855) 338-8359 or orders@sunburypress.com.

To request one of our authors for speaking engagements or book signings, please contact Sunbury Press Publicity Dept. at publicity@sunburypress.com.

FIRST CATAMOUNT PRESS EDITION: September 2021

Set in Adobe Garamond | Interior design by Crystal Devine.

Publisher's Cataloging-in-Publication Data
Names: PJ Piccirillo, et al.
Title: Northern appalachia review volume 2.
Description: First trade paperback edition. | Mechanicsburg, PA : Catamount Press, 2021.
Summary: An academic literary journal focused on writers from the northern appalachia region.
Identifiers: ISBN: 978-1-62006-869-4 (softcover).
Subjects: FICTION / Anthologies | LITERARY COLLECTIONS / American / General | FICTION / Cultural Heritage.

Product of the United States of America
0 1 1 2 3 5 8 13 21 34 55

Continue the Enlightenment!

Northern Appalachia Review

The Northern Appalachia Review publishes once annually. U.S. subscription rate is $15 for one copy. See submissions guidelines at NorthernAppReview.com. Address all correspondence to The Editors, generalinquiries@NorthernAppReview.com.

CONTENTS

INTRODUCTION

The team behind the *Northern Appalachia Review* works to honor the creative talent of our contributors by giving this book a shape that enlarges their work.

However successful we are at this owes to how much we facilitate a collaboration of ideas among our staff of readers, coordinators, and editors.

Our means for combining brainpower over the past year probably sounds familiar to you—evening Zoom calls. No matter what some of us think of the new medium, it enables representatives from all corners of our literary map to contribute to the format of this publication.

Early in our planning, conversation led to the idea of transformation in northern Appalachia, each of us having experienced some shade of it over the past several years. A lot of meetings and emails on the subject followed. We felt we were on to something. Come time to publish the call for submissions, we put it to our submitters to mull the idea.

We didn't force the issue, allowing general submissions. Even so, when the work came in, we saw everyone grappling in one way or another with transformation.

Laying it all before us, we realized by the very prevalence of the subject that it is indeed pertinent to the northern Appalachia experience. And the individual pieces revealed how transformation meant many things to our people.

The guiding question had to be, "What is the work telling us?" From there, we'd arrange it to add to that meaning. Each staff member chimed in on this, impressions built on expressions. Could we make better sense of the message by assembling the material in terms of past, present and future? No, too simplistic, not at all equal to the sophistication of what our contributors had given us. And then, through that serendipity of bright and enthusiastic minds at work, three words surfaced, the vertebral coherence we were looking for. Time. Place. Self.

Our genre readers and editors agreed that each piece spoke to at least one category. Not always expressly, sometimes obliquely.

And so you have an explanation for the focus of this edition of your Northern Appalachia Review. At least as much as I can offer—its meaning speaks through the remarkable work that follows.

PJ Piccirillo
Founding Editor
Editor-in-Chief

TIME

You will have to leave, so that I can return to you

An Uncle's Gift

We were born in the year of Watergate, though you and the world didn't know it yet, and Nixon would go on to win in a landslide. The Vietnam War was "winding down," though there were still many Americans and many Vietnamese dying, and they would keep dying for several more years. The country was at a low point and it was only going to get worse once the truths of Watergate and Vietnam came out and gas prices soared. These were ominous times to be born into, but our birth itself had nothing to do with that despair and everything to do with heroic sacrifice, hope, and love. Now you're young and misty-eyed enough that you probably do think your life is heroic, but trust me - that fades. Yet when it does, remember this: Somewhere amidst all the sweat and blood of Vietnam, one day destiny pointed its crooked finger at our uncle and called his name.

As you know, dad never served in Vietnam, despite being drafted in 1968. The first time he was called in he was too skinny, barely a hundred pounds, so they rejected him, sent him back to mom, who would unwittingly fatten him up, at least enough for the Army to accept him and set him on the training regimen for Vietnam. Dad got as far as Fort Polk, Louisiana, where it rained violently and you had to turn your boots upside down to make sure there were no scorpions inside. The next stop was Vietnam. But our dad was delivered from that fury.

Uncle Frank, who was a couple of years younger than dad and had no wife or kids, had enlisted in the Marine Corps, another poor boy off to fight a rich man's war, but if he was going to do it, it'd be on his terms, so he signed up. By the time dad was at Fort Polk, Uncle Frank had already served a tour of duty in Vietnam during the Tet Offensive.

He saw some hard times over there too, fighting at Da Nang and Khe Sanh - even won a purple heart. I'm not sure why, perhaps he knew too well the horror of it all, but he showed up one day at Fort Polk in the formal dress of a proud Marine. When the Army guys saw him coming, they let him have it until their commanding officer let them have it, "Can't you see this man has a purple heart? Show him some respect! You haven't even seen any combat." Well, our uncle came to deliver the news to dad that he would be going back to serve a second tour of duty, which, given the rules of combat that stated only one son could be in action at a time, meant in essence that he was taking our father's tour of duty. So instead of going to Vietnam, our father was stationed with the 2nd 39th artillery unit in serene Schweinfurt, Germany, about 150 miles south of Frankfurt, where he lived in a comfortable apartment with mom and Tammy, while our uncle returned to face the brutality of Vietnam.

We've always been told Uncle Frank did it because Tammy was already born and he didn't want dad taking any risks with a wife and child at home. That seems to be reason enough, no further explanation needed. Fortunately, Uncle Frank survived his second tour of duty. Who knows, maybe our father would have returned home from Vietnam unscathed. But I've paged through some of our uncle's war poetry—it's not light reading.

Although Uncle Frank has never said anything about this, dad has told us this story many times, though always just the facts, no emotion or commentary, no "That's what a good brother does. I owe him still." He saved dad's life, and therefore ours. What a gift for a brother, for an uncle to give. No one has thanked him. I'm not sure it's the type of thing you can thank somebody for. I think the way dad thanked his brother was by telling that story over and over to us until he knew it would become part of us, something beyond forgetfulness. One just has to ponder it in silence. I now understand our uncle's actions as a courageous act of hope. With the world falling apart all around him, our uncle recognized something worth risking his life for. That is deep down love in defiance of the bitterness of the age.

The Old House

There is this shadow of a memory I have kept through the decades, another story our parents and sister always told us about—the Old House in Scotrun. I never really cared for this story much as it wasn't about us; we just happened to be there. It's kind of like looking at your friends' vacation pictures—"The hotel in Cinque Terra was just lovely. They had these wonderful pastries at breakfast—what were they called, dear, cinque fromaggio?" Or when your friends bring up that great party that you missed—"Boy, remember that party at Larry's when we smashed all the plates doing the Greek dancing. That was the best night ever." And on and on it goes until you're watching the clock and looking for an exit. The Old House was the one memory that our sister had and we didn't, so we were always left out and begging them to explain what had been so great about the Old House anyway.

Well, everyone just loved the Old House on Babbling Brook Road— seriously that was the name of the road—an idyllic paradise, God's own creation. Mom, dad, and Tammy all thought it was grand. It was our first place of residence on this earth even though I can't remember it. We were born in late July and by the fall we had moved out. My question when they slip into this reverie has always been, "If it was so damn great, then why did we leave and move into this dumpy trailer?" The answer has always been some appeal to Necessity. "The rents was raised." "The landlord sold the place." "The owner died." Actually, it was a combination of the last two: the owner did die, and then his son sold the place.

But this story taught us a few things about growing up in Northeast Appalachia, though I'm not certain they're true—nonetheless, we've considered them to be. The first is that anything good can vanish like sand out of your hands. We all know this. Everything changes, everything is impermanent but God in heaven. For some people this is learned late in life—a job one had for twenty years is suddenly lost, a spouse of thirty years dies—but you learned the fragile nature of good things young. I may be sounding like your parent, but this kind of heartbreak has to happen only once in life for you to begin to create an emotional detachment to the things and people around you. Fight that. There is an innocence you should hang on to, however foolish it may feel. It is worth caring about the things you want to love, perhaps those things most of all.

For some this lesson of impermanence becomes a lesson in pessimism, which you'll see all too often around you. This pessimism pervaded our end of Appalachia like an endemic sickness. "Is the hot water heater broke? Goddamn it, what's next? Well, we can just heat water on the stove for baths." "Are they closing the plant and sending the jobs overseas? Well, what can you do? The rich get richer and the rest of us get poorer." You have to admit that there is a lot of empirical evidence that supports this worldview. Much of history bears out that the rich do get richer and the poor get poorer. Inequality has spread across the United States like a virus since the Great Recession (kind of like your grandparents' Great Depression, but they didn't want us to think it was that bad, so they gave it a different name). That's just an indisputable fact.

There's good reason for accepting all this; it can save one hours of uselessly banging one's head against a wall. If you lose your trailer to fire or a house to foreclosure, perhaps it is better to chalk it up to God's will rather than question the justice of the U.S. banking system or the shoddy craftsmanship of most trailers. More than one person has been driven to despair pondering such things. After all, it was a historical fact that we moved out of the Old House, and we had little choice in the matter. Who's to blame for that?

Besides, you're going to grow up wasting a lot of time and energy raging about living in a leaky trailer with no hot water (you still have a few more years of that—well into junior high). There are only so many battles most of us can fight in a day. I'm not suggesting that you should live your life with this acceptance of pessimism and necessity. I'm actually telling you not to, but I'm also letting you know that it can be a good place to rest on a hard day. Don't harshly judge others for spending more time there.

Those stories about the Old House made me feel that things were always better in the past. A trailer with our parents and sister is the only place we're gonna live until we go off to college. But here they'd had this wonderful house in the mountains with a garden and land to spare. Why didn't we even get the memory of that? Why did we only get the shame of losing it? We were only three months old, and already we were living after the fall.

Now we've come to learn that not everything was better in the old days. And we need to be careful about our nostalgia for them; people will look to exploit that. As a nation, you'll learn, we tend to idolize the 1950s. Some things were good back then. There were unions and good paying jobs. But we also had segregation, and women were locked out of many professions and the best schools along with much else. And, unfortunately, you can't pick the past apart like that, not even your own; it's all one thing, the sublime and the horrific.

No, there'll be no going back to the Old House, Tommy, no matter how big a yard it had, besides that garden was full of rocks and weeds anyway.

This Side of the River

These recollections and sentiments about uncles and old houses are true. I'm glad to know you carry them with you. Yet you spend less and less time around here every year, so I'm not surprised that you have forgotten about my joy. To understand that, I will need to map out some things for you. We grew up in the eastern part of the Poconos, in Minisink Hills, Monroe County, Pennsylvania, on River Road between Shawnee-on-the-Delaware and Delaware Water Gap, where today the Appalachian Trail passes from Pennsylvania to New Jersey. They're small villages themselves, but of greater antiquity and prosperity then our Minisink Hills. The Minsi of the Lenni-Lenape nation first inhabited this land. Our little village along the Delaware, Minisink Hills, took its name from the Minsi, for this area along the River was the heartland of the Minsi. Minisink seems to mean "at the island," though some scholars once suggested it could mean "stone" or "mountain." The Minsi also gave their name to Mt. Minsi, our sentinel on the Pennsylvania side of the Delaware Water Gap. The name Minisink Hills was actually not formalized until the 1930s, less than 100 years; prior to that the place held a variety of names, such as Branchville, North Water Gap, and originally Experiment Mills, which came from the innovative flour mill along the Brodhead River, now a paper mill and Minisink Hills' only industry of note.

The first European to settle the area was Nicholas Depuy, an exile from Louis XIV's persecution of the Huguenots—French Protestants—he "bought" up 3,000 acres along the Delaware from the Minsi. Needless to say, the peaceful beginnings to European settlement did not last, and through various conflicts the Europeans killed, drove out, and stripped the Minsi of their identity. Settlers of various ethnic and religious groups—Dutch, German, English, Methodists and Moravians—displaced them. For over a hundred years, one of these families, the Eilenbergers, dominated our neck of the woods at the intersection of Gap View Drive and River Road where they had built the Eilenberger lumber mill, long since gone by our time. Across the crick from us still lived their descendant, an old lady always known to me simply as Mrs. Eilenberger.

Our trailer park where we lived until we were fifteen was about a half-mile from the Delaware River just over the hill. The public buildings consisted of a post office, all the way down at the dead-end of the aptly named Post Office Road, the venerable Minisink Hotel, a bar really more than a hotel, at the corner of River Road and Post Office Road, where we never went and were never to go, a Lutheran church across the street and up the hill, a perfect mountain church, where we also never went (it was all the way at the top of the hill after all), and oddly enough Carmen's roller rink, which we could go to and all the kids did, but we didn't really, only once or twice. We never went into three of the four public establishments in Minisink Hills, the one exception being the post office where we would walk in the warmer months. I don't know whether it was the paper or the aged wood, but there was something about the post office that smelled antique, like it had always been there, primordial. All else was woods, houses, roads, streams, and our trailer park.

You want to know where I found joy? Well, I found it all around me. In your mid-twenties you were taught the wisdom that God is found in all things and people, and you thought you really discovered something. And you did, but let me remind you that you already knew that when you were 10; you just forgot it. We had everything we needed, and none of it had to do with any of these buildings.

Well, there was this one building up the hill on River Road, our school, Smithfield Elementary. I count it a real blessing to grow up within walking distance of our school. That school was a haven. An easy walk up the hill, and we were met with sprawling fields for baseball, football, sledding in the winter, two sets of swings and monkey bars, and lots of empty roads for riding bikes around. Our friends and family spent hours and hours, whole days in the summer, with this private leisure park of ours.

You remember that one time up there with mom and dad on a cold snowy day? Dad and us were having a blast sledding down the hill. We had one of those old wooden sleds that you could steer at the front. We were always trying to find ways to go faster and see how far we could ride onto the field at the bottom of the hill—the fence at the end of the schoolyard was the elusive goal. Well, we decided to keep moving our sled higher up into the trees on the hillside to get an advantage. This worked well enough except that there were trees of course. We persuaded dad to get on our old sled with us. He agreed, and we had a few good runs like this, until we didn't. One time, the last time that day, we failed to navigate our way past the trees, and we hit hard into one of them. We went flying. Mom, who had been watching all of this at a distance, flew into a fury. Dad had hell to pay every time we got banged up on account of our playing hard, usually at our insistence. This time was no different. The wreck had brought a sudden halt to the sledding for the day, and as we walked our way down River Road, mom let him have it, "Thomas, you need to be more careful. Don't you think? You should have known that was a bad idea, going up into those trees." I kept my mouth shut but knew in my head that it was all our fault. Moreover, dad had got the worst of it. We were relatively unscathed, but he had really scraped up his shin on the tree and had quite a cut. He bore it all stoically, both the scrape and the scolding.

This land itself has its own blessings, especially the hills and the crick. Marshall's Creek to be exact, starting up in Otter Lake, ran directly behind the trailer park on its way to meet up with the Brodhead for a short spell and then the Delaware River. We spent entire summers in that crick. We never needed to go into East Stroudsburg to the pool at Dansbury Park, though we would occasionally for the novelty of it. The steady rolling of that crick was the silent and constant music of our youth. Most months and years, it ran in its beds, but it could be an angry crick. When the skies poured out their rain, that crick would angrily storm by and overflow its banks until the twenty feet between our trailer and the crick would dwindle to a handful. In our time there, it would never get as far as our trailer, which was the closest of them to the crick, but years after you left, that crick would be the end of our trailer park. In the flooding of 2004, the crick, like many of the others in the area, had grown strong from all the storms and raged through the trailer park and all Minisink Hills. The trailer park would be no more. Everything was damaged and all those who once called it home had to move on, including Tammy's in-laws, who had moved into our trailer after we had moved out. The whole area along River Road from our trailer park to Delaware Water Gap was under water. You were not there to see the destruction, but if you walk down there today you can still see the trailer park's absence. Mrs. Coco's house, rebuilt by the Leonards after the fire, is the only building on the property now, though one can still discern on the ground the traces of where the trailers had been.

We could measure and survey this land as others have. Route 80 runs right through the Poconos, which are roughly bordered to the South by the Blue Mountains and the Lehigh Valley where once they worked that Bethlehem Steel, to the West by Interstate 81 and the Schuylkill River where the coal country of the Wyoming Valley begins, to the north Interstate 84 and Lake Wallenpaupack well before you come to the dormant mines of Scranton and Wilkes-Barre and the New York State line, to the East the Delaware River and beyond it Jersey, the City, and the Shore. That was our world—Monroe, Pike, and Wayne counties with a few gleaming towns on the other side of their mountains and rivers.

But these are just geographic boundaries and place names. Geography is about more than lines on a cartographer's map. Even the best topographical map can't tell you how your stomach will rise and fall like you're on a rollercoaster while riding in the backseat of your father's car on Route 715 to Henryville. To know how muddy the shores of the Delaware are, you need to walk along them and push your foot heel into the wet sand until the water seeps up from below.

In the Poconos, all four seasons get a chance to display their full glory. The winters are cold and snowy. And we weren't daunted by them; we reveled in them. It was a rare winter day that saw gloves on our hands or a hat on our head. Sometimes the winters don't yield until mid-April, but once they do the springs stretch far into the summer and are filled with raucous thunderstorms and a hundred shades of green. Before you found out mom's favorite color was blue and switched it, our favorite color was once green, no doubt on account of all the variegated hues we saw all around us. The summers are long and lazy and can be quite cool, until the humidity hits like a sweaty slap in the face. Then you're in the dog days and the only relief is in the nearest crick or pool. But Autumn is a miracle. All those greens turn to yellow, red, orange, and brown of too many varieties for the painter's brush to recreate or the camera's lens to capture. Sunset in Autumn lights up the sky and hills like the first day of creation.

All of these seasons brought their visitors with them. Skiers in the winter, honeymooners in the late spring, families in the summer, and foliage tourists in the Autumn. We'd be stuck in traffic some blustery Autumn weekend, and you'd start ranting, "Why do all these people come here? There's nothing to see." Dad would sagaciously respond, "They come for the leaves. You can't see this in New York City." Well, that sounded like the stupidest reason ever. Like much else, you would come to understand this only from its absence and distance.

No, we weren't coal country, and that might confuse you a bit given outside perceptions of Appalachia—remember, there's lots of diversity in Appalachia; not everyone's dad's a coal miner, though that's a fine thing to be. The anthracite rich coalfields of Pennsylvania started the next county over, aptly named Carbon County; places like Hazelton and Mauch Chunk don't likely consider themselves part of the Poconos. Mauch Chunk, now that's where the Molly Maguires, who spent the

1870's organizing the Irish coal miners, were tried, framed, and hung. In order to keep the peace during the execution the state militia had to surround the county jail in Mauch Chunk, where you can still go today and stand in the hall where they were executed. Or you can check out the Sean Connery movie, *The Molly Maguires*, filmed right there in Weatherly at the Eckley Miners Village a bit up the road from Mauch Chunk. I don't think anything that interesting ever happened at our courthouse, aside from when the Strunk Boys of Henryville were finally caught and brought to justice for robbing and pillaging the neighborhood.

The Poconos are a liminal place standing between that Pennsylvania coal country to the west and Jersey to the east. As a result, the Poconos have come to possess a muddled identity, an uncertainty not unbecoming to our own boyhood demeanor. There were not enough city folk to make it urbane, but fewer longtime residents to conjure up images of the Appalachia of West Virginia and Kentucky. When our parents were young, and even still, when we were young, the Poconos were much more rural than they are today. People made their homes in the mountains and along the rivers and made their living farming, hunting, fishing or working in the various factories—the pocketbook factory (where our grandfather once worked), Hughes' Printing Company (where our parents met), Kulp's Foundry, McGraw Edison (where dad worked), and Patterson Kelly (where our brother-in-law would work until his death)— these were just a few of the factories that would enter into our childhood vernacular, most long since faded from the landscape of our youth.

The Poconos, however, are only an hour's drive from New York City, so for a long time they were a vacation spot for the well to do cityfolk, somewhat akin to the Catskills, our more famous cousins a short drive to the north. All these visitors needed places to stay: Tamiment, Shawnee Inn, Fernwood, Caesar's Pocono Resorts, Skytop, Unity House, Pocmont, Pocono Manor, Penn Hills, Mount Airy Lodge, just to name a few that were prominent in our youth. Tamiment for decades had a dining room—the Celebrity House—with all their famous guests emblazoned on the walls, something you only do once the celebrities stop coming. You once worked for the guy who invented the heart shaped tub, Morris

Wilkins, a legend in the Poconos. In Shawnee-on-the-Delaware, over the hill on River Road, Jackie Gleason and Arnold Palmer frequented the Shawnee Inn golf course. The Poconos could be glamorous, but the Poconos also remained stubbornly backwoods, such as down the hill in Minisink Hills where our trailer park was located.

Like most of the factories, many of those resorts have closed, as many of their former guests bought up time-shares and houses of their own in the Poconos—vacation houses many times, but also permanent residences as well. The hour/hour-and-a-half commute to New York City was seen as a slight inconvenience for the cheap land prices. This was all happening in the '80s and '90s as we were growing up and going through high school. All of our closest friends in high school were from outside the Poconos; most were from Jersey. For a while when you were in high school, our parents took up an extra job passing out flyers along routes 209 and 402 in Marshall's Creek advertising land for sale. I think the fellow they worked for ultimately went to jail for some kind of real estate fraud. It was a real boom town.

The locals have always felt ambivalent about all this. The resorts and the tourism created a lot of jobs over the decades, but the folks from the city brought their city ways, which often included a certain disdain for the locals and our trailer trash ways, and agonizing traffic, which choked roads that were meant for solitary cars. It was not uncommon to see the bumper sticker that read, "Don't like it here? Take 80 East." Most of all they brought with them their city money, which we liked and took readily, but it also meant higher prices for those with mountain money. It was the gentrification of the Poconos. The price of things like land or groceries shot up and often became out of reach for the locals. The house that seemed cheap to the New Yorker was way too expensive for the locals, many of whom consequently felt inferior to the new arrivals. You argued with your high school friends from out of state about the cost of their houses. You were always naively astonished at the price and thought them wealthy; they were always naively astonished at the price and thought themselves poor for having to move to the Poconos rather than Long Island.

Opinions on these matters were hard felt and ran the spectrum. As for us, aside from the traffic, we generally didn't mind the folks from New Jersey and New York. They made the Poconos a comparatively cosmopolitan place and they helped us from the mountains dream of other worlds. Moreover, people in the city needed what we had to offer too: hills and hills of trees filled with deer, wild turkey, and the occasional brown bear, and lots of peace and quiet. I just wish they weren't so intent on tearing it all down.

Appalachia

You need to say it. Appalachia. You owe it to me to say that you are from this place and I'm glad to know that you can now. Yet even that will raise questions for you. How should we say it? Appa-lat-cha or Appa-lay-shuh? Or is it one of the three or four other variations? It's a big place, so no wonder there's a bunch of ways to pronounce it. Some would say that how you answer this question determines whether you're from Appalachia or not. Of such things I'm not sure. I tend to rebel against anyone who would draw such stark boundaries between who is in and who is out. I don't doubt that Appa-lat-cha may be the more correct pronunciation, but where we're from it's Appa-lay-shuh, and if you're going to be true to yourself that's how you're gonna have to say it. I certainly don't mind if someone from West Virginia wants to tussle with me about the authentic way to say Appalachia, but you'll usually find that many folks throughout Appalachia don't give a damn how we pronounce our words, generally tired as they are with other people telling them how to pronounce their words. Typically, you'll be corrected for your pronunciation of Appa-lay-shuh more by people from Chicago, Seattle, and Boston, who, when you tell them you're from Appalachia, will say something like "No, you're not from Appa-lat-cha, you didn't say it right." At such moments, it'll be hard to tell if they're calling you out as a fraud or mocking our brothers and sisters who pronounce it differently. Either way, they're just carrying on the tradition of telling us how to speak.

Let me explain some reasons why you took so long to say you were from a trailer park in Northeast Appalachia. For some, Appalachia is a strictly defined geographic area on a map, determined by the Appalachian Regional Commission, and indeed Monroe County, Pennsylvania is in that geographic boundary—a border county to be sure. Still, growing up we never thought of ourselves as being from Appalachia. We were just from the place we were from—like the birds who don't recognize the air they fly in or the fish who don't sense the water around them. Sure, there were hints, like the hillsides full of mountain laurel, the Appalachian Trail passing a mile or two from our trailer park, but no, you didn't know we had come from Appalachia until you moved away. When you return to the Poconos with your future wife, a Michigan native, she'll be struck by the people, including our family, and our attitudes, the things we see as possible and impossible, the ever-present pessimism and distrust in the system, whatever it be—education, government, business—that it's all stacked against us. You'll be resistant to this idea at first, but you'll slowly come to recognize its truth. You, too, lived in a trailer with no hot water, had a dad who worked in a factory and a mom who held odd jobs; we wore second-hand clothes, and you still have the bad teeth to show for it. And besides, we grew up surrounded by the Appalachian Mountains—where the hell did you think you were from?

Yeah, I get it, the Poconos are a liminal place—cross the county line to the East, the Delaware River, and you ain't in Appalachia anymore. So while we were Appalachian, there were plenty of people around us who weren't. I hate to present it so starkly, but there are really two Poconos. There are the Poconos full of tourists and honeymooners and city-folks from east of the River. I suspect that one could come to the Poconos, just look at the pretty mountains and surround yourself with folks from the eastern side of the River, and never know that you were in Appalachia. But there is an underground to that world, and that's where you lived. The folks in the Poconos who cook in the diners and work behind the registers in the gas stations, who bag the groceries and make up the rooms at the hotels and collect the trash—these folks are from Appalachia.

Even more, if you're a kid from a borderline place like the Poconos and you can choose either to pretend to be in with the urbane folks from the east bank of the River or to confess to be among the crowd of poor, under-educated folks from the west bank of the River, what are you going to choose? Most likely you're going to choose the lie over the truth; you're going to choose to pretend to be something you're not, to laugh at the jokes about the hillbillies, and to glamorize everything from east of the River. We were brought up that Appalachia was some other place, a place where poor and lazy hillbillies sat around drinking whisky and brawling while their neglected kids played around the yard half-dressed. No, we weren't hillbillies; we weren't white trash. We thought those terms described other people we had never seen or met. For us to embrace them would have meant that everything other people said about them could be said about us. So we ran from all that—our second-hand clothes, our trailer park, our identity—and tried to be something we weren't—middle-class Americans. It was a great labor to discover that we were from Appalachia. You had to leave so that I could return to you with this truth. If you want to know how I found joy in a trailer park, you will need to ruminate on that. And perhaps ask yourself—What else do you need to move away from so that you can see it?

Marriage Mirroring a Geography of Pennsylvania

What Our Ancestors Found:

A virgin forest of the seventeenth century: unshaped.
No flat land; only the most fertile,

seeding children on the honeymoon
unforested wilds spread out in bold glory.

Untrusted; the woods cleared by natives.
As pioneers we'd rather break our backs ourselves,

All the years of bending to convention—
only to find the valley's soil was as limited as the horizon
and did not trail up the hills, like all the fits and starts of a life.

Abandoned. The pastures became forest again.
We've reached our high-water mark for clearing the forest—
it was 100 years ago.

It was mid-marriage, kids, and looking forward to the visits from
grandparents to show them the latest, new flip onto the baby's back,
the steps, the walking, even sitting up was enough.

Now, in Latrobe, where turkeys roam and are shot,
deer hunters fall back, surprised to stumble across stone walls
and barbed wire of the past.

—the same way I feel
when my computer boots up and displays
all the old pictures of my phone—
pictures of blonde toddlers,
miles of summer rides to your heartland roots.

Our pioneering ways produced much good soil—
    Children of the earth.
Miles from roads or neighbors,
    creating new spaces over old woods.

A Series of Poems with "Found Language" credited to A Geography of Pennsylvania,
E. Willard Miller, Penn State University Press

Because My Uncle Was Allergic

We were paid to kill
anything that buzzed,
each crushed carcass,
hornet and honeybee alike,
worth one penny.

We dumped the pickle jars
out on the porch.
Our parents counted the bodies.
It takes a thick layer of bees
to make a dollar.

That was a long time ago.
Remorse is pointless.

Here in the suburbs,
nothing hums. Unvisited clover
flecks the perpetual lawns,
tiny markers as the light
fades.

Elegy for Mitchell

We were sprawled across a cool, concrete porch floor;
our softball game over, our thirst quenched
from a garden hose, when we learned that you had died.

A boy, a few years older than I, broke the news;
repeated secondhand what his mother had told him that morning.
A solemn kid, he handled the news gently, as if it were a baby bird
needing room to flutter before settling.

We fidgeted, looked everywhere but at one another;
I blinked back tears, afraid of ridicule,
unsure of proper protocol without my mother's guidance.

I watched an ant wrestle a transparent fly wing across the floor,
listened as a murmuration of starlings gathered in the maples,
seeking comfort in multitude.

Finally, someone looked up and said you were a nice boy,
a good outfielder. I recalled your A's in third grade arithmetic.
A boy told one of your silly jokes and I laughed until my stomach
    hurt.

We showered you with accolades until the shrill afternoon whistle
carried across the Licking River Valley from Burnham Boiler,
released us from our elegy and called us home to dinner.

The starlings, too, acknowledged the whistle's directive and
rose from the maples; their flight, a choreographed running stitch
darning a shadow across the sun.

Above us—the riotous din of call & wing—so deafening,
that racing down the back alley toward home, I could barely hear
my own shouts and laughter rising to join the revelry.

Sugar Maple

Maybe 200 years is too long to wait for love.

Mother is gone now, and many children, too. So many years have passed, all those years that ask questions into the bald and brazen silence. Heart can be harder to come by than you think when you're first reaching up into the sunlight.

There's a trail that runs beside me. It's older than I am. For tens of thousands of years, it was buffalo who took the path of least resistance down the side of this hill to the water below, and then deer would pick up behind them, nibbling at tender roots broken or upturned by heavier hooves. People eventually followed the path already made. Mostly hunters, their steps soft and calculated. A family or two made camp nearby. I once had a boy.

He took shelter here, buried his treasure just near my feet. Smooth stones from the river. A sliver of metal. A handsome turkey feather. He was just a wee thing, a few feet tall when I first met him. For a while, we took comfort in each other. He'd lean his backbone against mine, tap his foot, and sing out to the birds, imitating them and waiting for their reply. He fooled them a time or two, his bright laughter, my new sunlight.

A winter passed and I didn't see him. Sure enough, when the robins returned, so did he, with more lank and more treasure. A shard of glass this time. Another smooth stone from the river. The ground was still hard and cold when he unearthed his stash to bury the new goods.

I'll keep them safe.

Until one day. A woman's voice, his mother's cry, sharp with fear, rang out through the woods. He curled up behind me, hiding. I could feel his smile. I couldn't tell him it was not the time to play, even though I heard the alarm sound in his mother's tone. Danger.

Go, boy.

I willed him to hear me, but he didn't move.

Not far behind her, other voices broke through, unconcerned, ominous. Men. Foreign. Strangers to this path. The boy's body, on instinct, froze against me, his breath hot and halting. They took their time passing, me a great hulking cloak of invisibility, their eyes taking stock as they strolled and surveyed all the way to the water below. The timber to be sheared. The wealth waiting deep underground. The water that could be used up in so many ways. It was hours before the boy's heartbeat slowed to a normal pace. Knowingly, he took most of his cache with him when he left, without making a sound, just before dark. He realized what I didn't then: No treasure was safe anymore. These strangers would find and take. My little runaway. I hope he met up with his mother. I hope she held him tightly. I hope he found armloads of river rocks and put them to good use, built a fortress around himself.

I'll hope that forever.

I never saw him again.

From there, the world changed. Not just for me. Things sped and reshaped. The forest thinned, not as badly here as in other places. Other places were struck down, stripped, and gutted.

For me, the song of spring still came, the same as it always had. The stirring, above and below. The showers that awaken everything, bring the cool green mosses and the slick seas of ferns. As always, the water flowed and snaked down, building from a trickle to a gurgle, down, down toward the meadow below—but suddenly, without warning, it stopped where it once had kept moving. They had made themselves a playplace. Their own shelter in the woods. The strangers gathered here to escape.

The children's laughter. That was the best part. Splashing, squealing, yelping like pups in the distance. That never bothered me, personally, but I could feel the tug, the burden of trapped water on the earth, even from this distance. With every rain, the weight grew. The ground stretched and strained beneath it. They played, brought in their animals, their music, their merrymaking. Until the day their instruments and tools gave way. The whole damn thing came apart in waves. You don't see that often in the mountains, and I've seen a lot. I can't imagine what that kind of power—waters unleashed, full of rage—did to my family below or the rows of houses that had cropped up there, the workers the merrymakers had sent underground. I faded back into the background for some time, twice failed. Twice unable to offer protection. I thought I was old then.

At least the deer returned.

Hooves trampled down the fine fescue, dandelions, thistles. Quiet friends, revering the ancient trail. Raccoons and robins, louder, less noble, but still as welcome. I was without my boy, but I was still standing—and not alone. You're never alone in the woods, not if you're paying attention. I wasn't, for a time. Short summers, long ones. Winters in white and gray. They circled past with little participation from me. I grew as hardened as you might expect.

Then, after decades, the Great Ruckus. The forest was suddenly worthy of notice again. First, the surveyors came. Next, ten men wearing blue shirts and khaki pants worked backhoes, excavators, and timberjacks. They toiled for weeks, their worrisome tools gnawing away at stubborn earth and roots. Men in dark trench coats came behind them, massaging their beards, chests puffed, imagining they were first to stamp footprints across this path. Their hats amused me, made me wonder whether the boy ever grew to take on games like this, arranging comrades in line, each with a few words to say, each clearing his throat first.

I looked their way, but no one saw me watching. They had erected signs among my sisters and a couple of my older brothers. We all had a good chuckle at the names they chose; I tried not to take it personally that they didn't select me. *That's okay. I belong to the boy.* The fanfare came after that—steady for a while—and then dwindled down, returning us to a pleasant, peaceful place, for the most part. Years went by. People became preoccupied, which is nothing new. Their box of maps to match the signs along the trail was left to spiders. Just a few regulars remembered this path, so carefully laid. I resigned myself to watch the last of them.

That's when the whole world got sick, which was why these two newcomers covered their faces.

But a mask couldn't hide their laughter. I heard that first—a little too loud, nervous—from the picnic grounds 100 meters away. I eavesdropped. I couldn't help myself. My protective instinct, perhaps. These two didn't need saving, though, they needed seeing.

Playful, they stepped near me, moving quickly, aflutter. The girl was covering up the names of the trees while he made guesses at the type. More laughter, nerves, trembling. Those signs, their immediate distraction, are always first to catch attention when people wander this way. A second time through, though, and a miracle happened: They looked right at me.

I mean it. They knew I was there.

They made sure I knew that they knew. One early morning he—the man who hadn't lost his boy heart—came back, alone, and bowed to me. With a smile I recognized, he marked his treasure: He honored my space with a sign of my own. A game, perhaps, but isn't everything they do a dance of some sort? I will, for certain, play along.

They gave me something real. They bestowed on me what no one, not even my mother, had. They gave me a name. They were once a moment's notice, a fleeting glance, away from missing me, but now and forever I have a name.

He came back another day, with her on his arm this time, to show her. They were shifted by then, their spirits a little greener; they moved with care, hands entangled. Still that flash of excitement, their hearts beating like rabbits, their breath catching, tipsy with laughter—gentler this time though, their smiles slow and steady. Blossoming love. I reached out my boughs to them, a circle for their embrace. They gestured, arms wide, back to me and the frame I made for them to remember for always, a safe space, tucked away in the woods.

How much can a heart hold? Made bold by the woodlands, drunk on moss and bark, alive with the dead and living creatures beneath their feet, they're trying to measure it. Letters. Numbers. Signs. Ceremony. Trees. They count me, too. I hear them plotting, their holy mischief. I want to hold them tighter. One day, I will be a stump.

For now, I remain, watching them shape and conspire and dream and whirl. I've done my job. I'm an elder, a space maker, river rocks buried at my feet, a commemorative symbol erected before me. People sense it.

The pair, they come back to dance still, swaying slowly, responding to breezes the same way my younger branches do. Their heartbeats sync, sharing gentle kisses that I make record of in my bones, in these last few rings around this strange earth.

They have their own record-keeping, too. Maps and drawings and curious markings, like my boy so long ago, seeking treasure, seeking sanctum. Others arrive now, seeking too, following rituals those two ordained, the new ones understanding them in their own way. Their own games. Who can say what they see? I reach out my arms to them, to all of them, the way I did for the pair who saw each other, the ones who saw me. An embrace. A moment's refuge.

It's the best that I can give, my treasure returned to the world where nature planted me. I know I have only a few freezes and thaws left to go, a few hundred sunrises, but the sugar still shimmers in my veins. Maybe sweeter now than ever, for all the waiting.

Crow Counting

Social, inquisitive, mysterious,
always news to bring.
Count them:
One, omen for bad luck,
two predicts good fortune.

Crow messengers twist and turn
as each day spins to and from the light.
These are my people,
plain perhaps, among the elegant.

They are coming, count them:
three forecasts health,
four oracles prosperity.
Stop at four, anything further
brings more than you can imagine.

But have you seen them
in late April light? As they turn,
a hint of iridescent blue
flashes an ancient memory
deep in our bones.

Oxidant

You always hear people go on about how rust
looks like a river, but we can sit here and watch
it flow as night falls. The red-orange that looks
less brick than illness flows from behind walls,
under floors, hungry for a banquet offered only
when the sun, exhausted, abandons its endless
struggle against the mist. It drives down I-beams,
lockers, corrugated plate as if it followed
an invisible scalpel, a point at the front, ever-
widening behind until every last surface
is pocked, pitted, so loaded the rust becomes
a liquid, drips to the tile floor and vanishes
in a puff of silver mist. What holds this derelict
building together we do not know, but for it
we are thankful. We do not take it for granted,
however. We are still, as calm as can be
with the sounds of feet outside, sometimes
a scamper, sometimes a march, the worst
times a soft tread, slow, the kind you hear
just before the door is kicked in. But
the rust is loud, the rust is bright, the rust
gets in your eyes and nose and anyone
who searches for prey needs other, greater
senses. So we wait, we offer rust
(for we have nothing else) to the stars,
and when the iron and steel begins
to shine again, we can emerge,
and the battle is once again joined.

Train Engineer John Hess's Last Day

East Conemaugh, 1906

The river still rises in my dreams,
and we fly down the tracks just ahead
of the wave that engulfed the city.

I race my engine, breakneck,
sounding that long whistle all the way,
then startle awake, sweated and elated—
somehow my crew survived!

My engine was later restored.
I never would have believed it possible,
after seeing her tumbled on her side
with the other cars, like a bunch
of dead cows.

Seventeen years now since the great flood.
I close my eyes to this sick room, and clear
as my own wife's face, remember

    swinging up to the cab next to the fireman,
    checking the gauges and valves, seeing
    a good fire in the box, the gleam
    of the steel rail ahead. . .

I was one with that engine.
My hand on the throttle, feeling
the shudder of power beneath me,
steaming her down the line.

Now I hear a distant train's moan and chuff.
If only I could rise from this bed, walk
to the window, watch the white blast of steam,
the progress of engine, coach, caboose
like wind around the mountain bend.

Lost and Found

Michael got into his truck to begin the drive into town. He always liked the nineteen-mile trek down Hawks Run Road, through the cemetery, and on to Doug's Hardware. It was a peaceful and quiet ride, despite the occasional squeak of the rusted suspension in his old Ford Ranger as he weaved between gravel and divots where the runoffs from the stream had dried to dust after the rainy season. He rolled the windows down and let the mix of pollen and parched earth fill the cabin. As he took a sip of black coffee from his faded black travel mug, his mother's words echoed through his mind. "You're lucky you don't have allergies like me," she would say as she brought a tissue to dab the corners of her hazel eyes. The old Pittsburgh Steelers logo was nearly worn off, but it was the only thing he had left that reminded him of her, aside from a picture he had from her on the driver's side sun visor where it escorted him.

He loved that picture of her, with her wind-blown golden-brown hair loosely framing her face from beneath her tassel cap, the golden flecks of her eyes drawn out by the yellow in her hat juxtaposed against the stark white and gray backdrop of a Pennsylvania winter. They had gone to Erie for the day to walk out on the frozen lake and take family pictures. His father, Richard, managed to snap one test photo of his mother before he realized the battery hadn't been charged. Richard, prone to temper, began to curse and threw the camera to the ground, the lens popping off and rolling between his feet. Michael's mother had an elegant way of calming down his father; he remembered how she put her hand on his father's chest and told him to take a few deep breaths. The red in his cheeks, flushed from anger, gradually dulled to a pink lingering from the cold winds and he gave her a halfhearted smile. As Michael thought about that day, he mirrored his father's smirk as he brushed the dust off the lip of his mug and took another sip of coffee. He paused at the stop sign, closing his eyes to better visualize his memory, until he noticed the faint scent of Northern Pines in the distance.

The smell of the pines meant that Oakwood Cemetery was just around the corner. Michael avoided cemeteries at all cost; they were a constant reminder of all he had lost. The year after his mother went missing, Richard became despondent as his compulsion with finding his wife yielded no results. Richard became further withdrawn as he soaked his sorrows in whiskey to try to numb the pain and spiraled into lunacy. Believing the thought of living the rest of his life alone was worse than living at all, he left his 18-year-old son the family sorghum farm, along with the insurmountable debt it had acquired as he abandoned reality, and Michael. Orphaned and unable to take care of himself, let alone 100 acres of farmland and the mounting bills, Michael sold the property to pay off the debt. He took what little money was left to purchase a small cabin 20 miles outside of town, where he had lived in solitude for the last ten years. Unable to forgive his father for giving up hope and deserting him, Michael could not bring himself to visit his gravesite. Despite this, Michael became uncharacteristically happy when he passed through Oakwood. It meant that he only had one more mile to go before he would get to Doug's Hardware, which meant only one more mile until he could see her.

Michael fell in love with Maria Ezra the moment he first saw her warm smile greeting the customers at Doug's. He had gone there to post a newly laminated flyer of his mother on the "Missing Persons" bulletin board, but quickly became distracted the moment he saw Maria. He remembered her well from high school, although it had been several years since he had last seen her. Her rounded face had thinned out to reveal high cheekbones that complimented her strong nose. They had a few classes together, but as a shy child, he could never get enough courage to talk to her. By the time he built up the confidence to speak, her family moved across the county to a new school district in the city, and he figured he would never see her again. He hadn't, until that moment at Doug's that took the breath from his lungs.

Her lips were unnaturally pink for her dark complexion. He imagined they were stained pink from eating fresh strawberries from the farmer's market behind the hardware store. Her hair was shiny and dark, messy, like melted chocolate pouring out of her head to frame her face, but not even melted chocolate could compete with the sweetness of her smile. Every time he looked at Maria, his mother's words would enter his mind. "When are you going to bring home a nice girl," she would tease. "You know I want some grandbabies one day!"

Michael quickly found himself making excuses to visit Doug's as often as possible. Every time he saw Maria his heart raced, clouding his thoughts and drying his mouth to match the dirt road he drove in on. When he opened his mouth to speak, his vocal cords would tighten and he couldn't even manage to pass the air needed to say the word hello. He would just walk past her and roam around the store aimlessly, picking up a few things here and there, pretending to need things to fix up the house. He would just stare at the entranceway where she would remain until he left the store again.

"What are we fixing up this week, Mikey?" Doug would ask him. Michael would get red in the face and wipe the sweat off his brow with the sleeve of his green and black flannel shirt; he was never good at lying, but he would make up some story about how his sink was leaking. Doug always showed him the specials on plumbing hardware and Michael, too polite to turn down Doug's kindness, always bought whatever Doug thought he needed to repair his bathroom fixtures. Every week after he made his purchase, he walked past his dream girl whispering, "Bye Maria," so that no one heard him, and every time he left she smiled at him like she always did.

Every night Michael envisioned them together, their silhouettes dancing beneath the glow of the moonlight on the patio outside of his cabin by the lake. There they would stay until the sun rose to illuminate the waters, their bodies moving in perfect harmony to nothing but the sweet song of the waves crashing onto shore. He would embrace her curves, holding onto her hips like they were the key to immortality, and she would lay her head upon his chest looking up at him with her beautiful brown eyes, her locks falling over his shoulder to gently tickle his neck. "My mother would have loved you," he would imagine himself whispering to her as she fell asleep in his arms.

The few friends Michael had left called him crazy, obsessed even, to think that his fantasy of loving Maria would ever become a reality when he couldn't even speak to her. At first, they were sympathetic towards his impractical desire, but as time went on they grew tired of his infatuation with her and soon began to worry about him. "What would your dad think about this? Give it up, man" they would say. He reminded himself there was a reason he chose to live in isolation. "You're wrong," he would say as he described the way he would win her over. One day he would run into Maria, maybe walking on the outskirts of town. Her car would have broken down trying to get home, and he would offer her a ride. They would fall in love by the time they got to town and they would live happily ever after. "You need help, man," they said, but Michael didn't care.

As he passed the white marble mausoleum, guarded by twin seraphims mounted on each side of the door, he knew that he was nearing the end of Oakwood Cemetery. Whether it was excitement or anxiety, the sweat began pouring from his face, his heart pumping so hard you could see the veins in his neck pulsating in and out. Michael exited the cemetery between the two monumental oak trees framing the road into town. He took a few deep breaths to calm down while he waited at the red light and continued to make the first left into the parking lot of Doug's Hardware.

He walked through the door expecting to see Maria's smiling face, but today something was amiss; he was not greeted by the radiant smile that he had been longing all week to see. He paused in the entrance way of the store and slowly turned his head towards the empty space that she usually resided in. He stood perplexed, engaged by what could not be. Noticing Michael, Doug shouted from across the room, "Need to fix the sink again I suppose?" Michael snapped out of his trance.

"Doug… Where is Maria Ezra?" he asked, clenching his fists to keep his hands from shaking. Doug furrowed his eyebrows trying to recall her. "You know," Michael said, staring at the bulletin board, his face drained of color, "Maria Ezra, about five and a half feet, big brown eyes, dark curly hair. Her picture has been here for months."

"Oh, yeah," Doug remembered. "We don't keep the pictures up after they're found." Michael felt a surge of energy rush through his body. He couldn't believe after missing for months that she had finally turned up. He looked above the empty space Maria used to fill, at the picture of his mother, elated by the thought of how happy she would be for him that he could finally live out his dreams. Michael's train of thought was interrupted by Doug's dismayed voice.

"Poor girl," he said. "They found her body a few towns over stuck in the dam. Police said she drowned."

Paid For

I held onto that car
too long, expensive beast,
AC no good,
electronics on the blink.

I'd been schooled
in how to keep things going,

my father washing out
plastic sandwich bags
and drying them until
they turned blind.

To the Future Owner of my 1910 American Foursquare House

Our house. This house with maple hardwood floors,
with a window of stained glass on the stair,
this house that feels solid, with oak doors,
this house that is the only thing we share,

was once a hole, a maw, an excavation,
a gaping chasm willed into the ground
and laid stone by stone for a foundation
that has stretched forward centuries and bound

me to you and you to me in dimensions
that neither you nor I can ever know,
creating ghosts of parallel intentions
to take the seedling of this house and grow

a life from my past into your present,
a life with rugs, with lamps, with kids, with spouse,
a life holding its breath, a life expectant
of being the sole owner of this house. Our house.

Don't Go into the Woods

Don't walk past the baseball field, the first stand of trees.
Avoid the scatter of rocks, uneven tar, loose gravel.
Don't scramble across the ledge of legless chairs, worn tires,
overturned barrels, broken beads of glass. Stay quiet.

The hillside opens up, stretches out, a graveyard of stolen cars,
scorched metal. The back half of an ice cream truck
submerged in mud, doors rusted open, reeks
of beer and mold and urine.

Ignore the brambles that reach for your shirt,
the thorns that snag at your thighs.
You hear a pickaxe strike concrete.
Plastic jugs, anchored along the sides of the creek,
gurgle and hiss. You know you should leave.

Just below the next rise, Old Man Lewis,
who is, in fact, not very old, built his house,
slate walkway, peaked windows,
porch roof painted a pale summer blue.

Old Man Lewis marches, sings cadence, paints signs
in black ink, circles and crosses that don't make any sense.
He wears his rifle strapped over his chest,
burrs stuck through his beard like pins in soft linen.
He weaves tripwire from fence posts through bushes and roots.
If you get too close, he aims, pulls the trigger,
birds and leaves scattering, and you run. Run.

You slap your breasts and stomach and legs,
searching for blood, out of breath, out of the woods,
doubling over, laughing.

Struck on the Road to Damascus

May 5, 2015
From charleshcabrizi@gmail.com to gregolson2100@hotmail.com
Greg—I drove through a little Appalachian Foothills town called Clement on my way to Columbus, Ohio last month for a photo shoot and made what I thought would be a quick stop at an ancient, red-brick bar on the main drag. It was full of talk about a man called George Libris, who apparently tried to run down his ex-wife's lawyer with a pickup truck. The lawyer ran too fast for him, though, more's the pity.

But anyway, I spent the evening talking to a local named David McGraw, an elderly long stick of a man, and he filled me with stories about George Libris and his clan. I thought one in particular was pretty interesting, so I'm sending it on to you in McGraw's own words, as well as I can remember. Of course, my words aren't nearly as good as yours, but hope you enjoy the story. Maybe you can use it in an article someday. Chuck

People in Shawnee County say the Libris family is plumb crazy, but I don't know. I'm their second cousin on the McGraw side, grew up with them, eleven kids in all, and while old George was always a champion drinker and professional wild man, his sisters and brothers weren't near as bad. Looking back, it just seems to me like all the Libris kids had some kind of secret weakness in them, and if they weren't careful, their weaknesses might break loose and turn their lives into living Hell. Just like everyone else in the world, I reckon. But like I said, they aren't all crazy. Hell, old Lonnie Libris even became a preacher after he got hit with the Holy Ghost about twenty-five years ago, back when he worked at Preston Bottling Company.

What's that? You never seen anyone get the Holy Ghost? Well, let me tell you then.

Lonnie musta been about twenty-eight, twenty-nine then, with a wife and two kids. A good-looking man with that slicked back black hair and black eyes, and a flirt too, but not nearly as bad as George, at least not then. Lonnie had some sense. Of course, he'd been raised Pentecostal, like the rest of the Libris', but after he left home and his mother, he wasn't much on church.

But just like Lonnie tells it in his fire and brimstone sermons, he walked out to his truck after work one hot August day, hungry and tired, when out of nowhere he hit the ground hard, struck by an internal lightning bolt. He'd been working late and most people had already left for the day, so it's hard to tell how long Lonnie lay on the black top before I found him. See, I worked there, too. There he was, face up beside his truck, eyes open and rolled back, making not a sound, just quivering a little. Hell, I thought he'd had an epileptic fit, and I didn't know whether to run back inside or to just start yelling for help. But right when I was getting ready to go back, Lonnie let out a moan, and I dropped to my knees beside him, out there on that hot black top. "Lonnie," I said, "are you OK? Can you move?" Old Lonnie didn't say anything, just kept letting out moans. But when I stood, he sat up real quick-like and grabbed my hand. His black eyes had gone back to normal, but with an awful expression in them. Like Lonnie'd seen a ghost.

"David," he whispered to me. "Davey, I have seen such sights." And then damned if Lonnie didn't throw back his head and laugh. "I have seen the Lord. The Lord came looking for me and spoke to me. Hallelujah! Hallelujah!" Lonnie squeezed my hand until it hurt. "My God, my God, my beautiful Jesus," he crooned.

"Lonnie, can you get up?" I asked him again. "Are you hurt?"

"I have never been happier," Lonnie said, smiling like a fool in the sun. And then he got to happy laughing again, looking like he was ready to float on up the highway, no truck needed. But he climbed inside it anyway, started his Chevy up, and drove away a changed man. From that day on, he was in church every chance he got, taking along Shirley and the boys and going to every Pentecostal revival he could find. I know his wife Shirley wasn't crazy about it, especially when she found out Lonnie was studying to become a preacher. Hell, Lonnie could barely read until he got saved, but after that, he would sit and read the Bible cover to cover. It was a miracle, but a miracle Shirley wasn't ready for. But she went along with him, didn't fight him over it, and before you knew it, Lonnie found a Pentecostal preacher to sponsor him and became an ordained minister of the Church. And Shirley became not just Mrs. Lonnie Libris, but Shirley Libris, Preacher's Wife. Ha! They could make a movie out of that. Shirley Detty had been just the tiniest, prettiest little blue-eyed thing when Lonnie married her. They were poor as church mice because Lord knows the Libris family didn't have any money, not with Pap Libris drinking and gambling and whoring it all away, and Shirley's family didn't have much more. But Lonnie and Shirley were happy for a long time. Still, it's like what I'm saying about weaknesses—Lonnie had an eye for love, and as Shirley plumped up with the years, he found it harder and harder to keep that eye just on her. Lonnie always did like a real slender build. But, believe it or not, Lonnie quit his good-paying job at the bottling plant to cut wood because in his own words, "There are just too many sinners and back-biters at work." Me, myself, I think there were just too many good-looking women. But to give Lonnie credit, he did his best to live a righteous man and stay true to Shirley and the Lord. As the Good Book says, "If thy right eye offend thee, cast it out." Well, Lonnie cast out the bottling plant and threw it away just as far as he could.

About ten years after he found the Holy Ghost, or, I dunno, maybe the Holy Ghost found him, Lonnie bought himself a country church with some donated money and a bank loan. See, Lonnie did really well with the wood cutting. He'd cut wood wherever he could get it and sell rick after rick to rich folks in Columbus to burn in their fireplaces.

About this time, he also began preaching a lot about "thoughts." "The thought" Lonnie would belt out behind his very own pulpit, "is as bad as the act. If you have the thought, you have committed the act. Huuuh! Sinners, repent of your sinful thoughts! Huuuuuuuh!" With each huuuuuh! Lonnie's head would snap forward and he'd pound the pulpit with his fist. Didn't that black hair just fly! Half his congregation would yell Amen! while the other half looked kind of sneaky at the carpet. And then after he'd worked folks up good, Brother Lonnie would bring on the music, the heart of every Pentecostal church, any Pentecostal church that I've ever been to, at least.

Mrs. Kelly Quick, a real tall, skinny, good-looking blond, would start playing her banjo while Lonnie finished up preaching, singing "I'll Fly Away," or "I Shall Not Be Moved," as Lonnie called sinners to the altar to be saved. Been years since I've heard either one sung, 'cause as you see, I've kinda back-slid, but I still remember the words.

Jesus is my Savior, I shall not be moved;
In His love and favor, I shall not be moved,
Just like a tree that's planted by the waters,
Lord, I shall not be moved.

In my Christ abiding, I shall not be moved;
In His love I'm hiding, I shall not be moved,
Just like a tree that's planted by the waters,
Lord, I shall not be moved.

If I trust Him ever, I shall not be moved;
He will fail me never, I shall not be moved,
Just like a tree that's planted by the waters,
Lord, I shall not be moved.

By ones and twos, folks came up to kneel at the altar while the already-saved ones gathered around them to pray. Pretty soon, sinners and saved all would start talking in tongues. *Ubdallah, ubdallah*, they'd wail. *Oh shanata paya, ooooooooh shanta payashaneeta. Ooooooooooooonduuuuuuuuuuula. Ooooooooooooondulla.* And then Lonnie would lay his hands on people and shout, "Jesus, save this sinner!" Then the sinners would shake and stagger on down to the floor where the deacons and such-like attended to them.

What's that? Naw, there wasn't no snake-handling going on in Lonnie's church. Where do you think you are, Son, West Virginia?

Now I never was one for talking in tongues, and plenty of people think it's fake, but I tell you the air in Lonnie's church would get practically blue with the Spirit while the tongue talking and soul saving went on. Of course, one time I did see a woman pull down her skirt where it rode up to her underwear after she passed out with the Holy Ghost, but I dunno, maybe that was a woman thing. But what I do know is the church would get thick with emotion, and then you had to look quick and hunker down in your seat in case one of those deacons or deaconettes decided to come back and drag you up the aisle. I used to hide in the back pew, right next to Lonnie's niece Iola, the one who hid on the floor every Sunday, reading Little Women. She'd bring that book and read it, lying on the carpet while all the preaching and singing and tongue talking went on. Hell, she'd read right through John and Mable Curtz racing down the aisle to run around the church, banging the screen door and hollering as they went. Read it while her mother, Lonnie's sister Irene, filmed the service.

What's that? You wanna know about the filming? Well, I'm gonna order another beer then 'cause I'm getting kinda dry. You say it's your treat? Thank you kindly.

Well, let's see, along about 1985, Lonnie had done gone and got the church on the Clement, Ohio Channel Two Cable TV station, not to mention the AM radio, and Iola's mommy would camcord the whole shebang every Sunday night for people to see. Of course, when folks heard about that, all kinds of people started coming to Lonnie's church, even ones like the Quicks, who used to think they had too much class to Holy Roll. Hell, who doesn't want to be on TV? Back in those days there wasn't no YouTube or reality television. So, Son, when I say that church was full, I mean, that church was full. And that good-looking Kelly Quick became another attraction. She had a right pretty singing voice, and she could make that banjo sing. She and Lonnie would sing hymns together, she on her banjo and Lonnie on his guitar (she was teaching him to play guitar by then, see) and they sounded good. Kelly being pretty and all didn't hurt none, either. And while they played and sang together, I would sometimes catch Shirley glaring at Kelly evil-like from the middle pew (I had a good view from that back pew). Shirley wasn't a fool, and from what she said after all the mess, had her suspicions long before anybody else in the church did—

Yes, you're right. Lonnie and Kelly had themselves an affair going on.

I allus thought it began about the time Lonnie started on with "the thought is the same as the act" sermons. The way I figure, Lonnie started thinking impure about that married woman, couldn't get her out of his head, she being so bright, and shapely, and all. And from the looks of it, Kelly musta had plenty of thoughts of her own about him. She started Lonnie on her special diet, got him off the sugar and Pepsi habit, got him to looking good. After that, they got to going around the nursing homes together, playing guitar and singing the old-time music the residents wanted to hear. Not to be crude an' all, but I'd say that Lonnie and Kelly musta started up another kind of playing after they drove away from the nursing homes, if you catch my drift, safe from their spouses' eyes, and that's what got Lonnie started on his Sunday evening spiels. I guess in his mind Lonnie thought, "You all are just as guilty as me 'cause I know the men in this church are thinking about how they'd like to sleep with this beauty. No difference between you and me. Like Saint Paul says, the thought is the same as the act.

I think that's how Lonnie justified the affair in my mind. Just like he'd say, "That's man's law, not God's," when he got caught trespassing on other peoples' land to hunt mushrooms. Or when he'd get picked up by the highway patrol for driving wood up to Columbus without car insurance. Of course, they'd stop him for a busted taillight or speeding or something, but they always ask about the car insurance now, so there was Lonnie, in traffic court again.

Yes, Lonnie had a knack for justifying things, just like the rest of us, I'd say. Just like I justify drinking in this bar 'cause I ain't got no wife at home anymore. Of course, half the reasons she's gone is because I wouldn't quit drinking in this bar. Ha! Life is a funny proposition, isn't it? And you probably got some justification, Chuck, for drinking in this bar tonight and getting late to your motel. Maybe there's even some truth in it. Most justifications, do. Ha! Now you're laughing!

But anyway, Lonnie and Kelly's affair came to a head after Kelly's husband Ted found out what was going on. It took him a while, of course, because he didn't go to church with his wife, wasn't about to set foot in some Holy Roller church. I'd seen him a couple times around town, though, a lean, bald-headed man, soft-spoken, but he looked like a hard nut to crack just the same. He'd come home from work to find some of Kelly's clothes missing out of their closet and a note left for him on the bed. Ted called Shirley, who was sitting quietly at home, thinking Lonnie and Kelly were out on one of their regular nursing home runs. Told Shirley that Lonnie and his wife were commencing to run away together. And yes, they had in fact started to run off, but something in Lonnie made him turn around his truck at the Kentucky line and bring Kelly back home, but not before Ted found the note. Who knows? Maybe God struck him again. But instead of screaming and carrying on and trying to half-choke the life out of their spouses, Shirley and Kelly's husband decide to be Christian and hold a civilized sit-down meeting later that week with Lonnie and Kelly at the Quick's home.

No. I shit you not.

So they hold this sob session, and Lonnie and Kelly admit to being in love with each other but agree to call everything off, maybe because Lonnie truly believes that "What God hath brought together, let no man put asunder," or maybe to keep Lonnie's reputation gold in the community. See, he was a respected township man by then, had even been invited to give the invocation at Evanston County High School graduation. That's a big deal around here, Son. But the damage had been done, anyway, because Ted told one of his friends what happened, and he told his friends, and those friends told friends, and pretty soon everyone in Bidwell Township and the greater area knew about the Bidwell Pentecostal Shenanigans. Old Lonnie finally had to stand up before the pulpit and admit to his congregation what he had done and, just like Jerry Falwell, ask for forgiveness.

It didn't do no good, though. Kelly wasn't at church anymore—Shirley and Ted made sure of that; the twanging banjo player disappeared, and with her, over half the congregation. Some left because they judged Lonnie and found him lacking in character. Some left because church wasn't fun anymore. Some left because they didn't want to be associated with Bidwell Pentecostal's disgraced preacher. There was also the tricky fact that about five years before, Lonnie had preached fire and brimstone at two fornicating members in his congregation, all but forcing them out the door. I guess some people felt that what was right for those sinners was just about right for Lonnie Libris.

The church finally dwindled down to about twenty people, mostly Lonnie's relatives. I hung on for awhile, but then I married my second wife Claudine, and she didn't want to go to some fornicating minister's church. Looking back, I shoulda dumped that woman then and there, but like Lonnie, I was Love's Fool.

From what I hear and from what he's told me, Lonnie's got his church up to over half-full over the years. He's never quite gotten over the stain of adultery, though. And of course, they don't film the services no more, and even if they did, well, there's YouTube and all that now. It's not the big deal it used to be. Safe to say he's never been invited to speak at Evanton High again.

What's that? Has he been behaving?

Well, there's been rumors over the years, about a sixteen-year-old girl and even another church woman, and where there's smoke there's fire, as they say. The Libris Family do have their weaknesses. But still, I don't know. It don't pay to listen to rumors. He's been picked up for trespassing a time or two, but the traffic violations have toned down since Lonnie retired from wood-cutting last year.

Shirley keeps with him, too, and that's something, but then again, she really doesn't have much choice. Where would Shirley go at her age? What would she do? And Lonnie always has his church and his revivals. He still has his radio station, and that keeps him going, too. Calls himself non-denominational, now, though, maybe because of the way the Pentecostals judged him even after he turned back his truck. But Lonnie's still in good with them! Guess if you're gonna walk with the Lord, you've got to forgive those who persecute you, at least, eventually.

It's a lot of fun and a little sad to think back to those days, now, all the people at Bidwell Pentecostal shouting Hallelujah! and that pretty woman standing up there playing the banjo. But I got to admit, I get a good laugh, sometimes, out of Lonnie's philosophy, or at least my interpretation of it: "Thinking sinful thoughts? Well, you might as well act on them 'cause you already done them anyway!"

In fact, that's what I told myself this afternoon: "Dave, you're thinking about drinking down with the sinners at Peppers' Bar tonight, so you might as well go do it." Ha! It's a curious philosophy, Son, but, at times it can be right fun.

Confession

"A confession has to be part of your new life."
—*Ludwig Wittgenstein*

Birds tossed into living room ceilings,
dogs run over in driveways
while tied to the backdoor steps,
cats (who knows where your father took them?),
fish flushed, ferrets stuffed
and placed on the mantel
or buried in Tupperware.
You improvised elaborate rituals,
eulogized an animal's better nature.
Still it hurt when the rabbit bit you
when you pulled it, crippled, from the backyard pen.
You suspected your neighbor, Dicky Thomas,
only to learn, years later, it was your brother.
People change, though some would argue
a child who injures a rabbit
will suffer redemption.
Tonight under palm trees and full-flower moon,
far from the steelworks of your childhood home,
your brother admits
he once witnessed the spirit relinquish the body,
a body that lived without malice
when he dropped a stone in the hutch.
And a seed that festered inside him took root,
blossomed like a thousand apologies.

Y City Girl

I know a thing or two about clay, my family tree sprouted
from that heavy, clotted stuff. Dad's father & clan of brothers—
tough, hot-tempered scrappers—clung together like a ball of clay,
took no bull as they worked the factories, potteries & mills.

For a time, Grandma fed a family of eight on wages
her husband earned stamping Mosaic tiles. Grandpa's pockets
clinked with inch-square, candy-colored ones—Appalachian Legos
for his grandkids—their pocked, waffle-ridged backsides
& minor imperfections invisible as a beauty queen's blemishes.

Rainbows of mismatched place settings, ceramic seconds &
rejects from the local potteries graced our tables. Come spring,
we carried love home to our mothers by the armfuls.
Bouquets of dandelions & daisies in chipped McCoy vases
graced our kitchen tables.

My family hadn't the money to buy the tiles that Dad,
my grandpa & uncles had made, but we admired their handiwork
showcased in the municipal buildings around town.

Neighbors with money enough to decorate
plastered every available surface with Mosaic tile in bubble gum hues,
a sign of wealth, if not taste.
If nature called while I played in the yard of a kid from a home of
     means,
I'd ask to use their bathroom rather than run home—
just to wallow in the experience of extravagance & pride.

Questions of the Passion

I am a boy in the basement
of my grandparents' house,
the weary Ohio slumping by,
ice-cakes, spills of oil,
tarred drift logs sinking.
Over there,
the coal furnace, fat with fire, its
gray mummied ducts, the washing
machine, blunt tub with a voice
like drowning and its frightful terrible mangle.
Piles of kindling lean like stacked bones against a wall.
On cobwebbed shelves, jarred pears and peaches,
the whole harvest darkening.
And what does the dusty camel cricket sing,
sprinking from corner to corner
in the coal cellar? What do the lifesaver
washers mean in their little
jars of oil? What connections
do the nails long to make? What turns
must the wrenches deploy? What rusty secrets
the tool box maintain? Where
is that broken sexton, custodian of dust?

I turn about and about
in the dimness, half-windows obscured
by lint and webs. Light like Good Friday
afternoon, Him on His cross, thirsty
and broken. What birds are those
I imagine on their wide, dangerous wings,

circling above this house by the river, what
questions arising that must be answered
but are not, what black stain on the floor,
spread out like a map,
wine-dark, slick as new spilled blood?

Appearance

Your mother speaks to me in a dream sometimes, she says to tell you
the purple irises you pulled from her garden after she died are not

getting enough sun and the constellation of beauty marks on your
   daughter's arm
stand for something only you will understand if you have the eyes to
   recognize.

She wants you to get your nose out of that book and put some music
   on,
go dancing, stay out until sunrise. In my dream, I hear her making
   coffee

in the kitchen with the metal percolator she used to keep on the
   stove, her hands
pulling the top and bottom apart to dig out the pieces of the filter,
   fitted inside

like a nesting doll and she keeps talking to me—running water in the
   kitchen sink,
rinsing the used coffee grounds down the drain. She wants me to pray

to the emblazoned Our Lady of Guadalupe with her eight-point stars,
   but all I can
muster is the eclipsing prayer of a blazing sun atop a darkened
   crescent moon.

I tell her I could never love you enough for her but she just keeps on
   talking, her voice
fading into the thrumping boil of the coffee pot percolating wildly on
   the stove.

A Pinkerton's Plight

Interview by Mina Moore

September 30, 1892
Pittsburgh, PA

In my research on what had happened in Homestead, Pennsylvania on July 6, 1892, I'd come to hear about a young man currently working for the Pinkerton Agency still living in the vicinity of Pittsburgh who had been involved in the riot. My editor was only too glad to send me to see if I might be able to get the man, who went by the name of Tom Ewing, to speak to me about what he'd experienced that day. He agreed to meet me for an interview at the B&O Station near the place known by the locals as The Point.

"What happened on the riverbank that day?" I asked, pen in hand.

He smirked ruefully. "Don't you know?"

"The papers were vague on that part."

"I s'pose they would be." Ewing took out a cigarette and lit it, taking a few puffs. "They want to gin up support for Amalgamated." His eyes focused somewhere in the distance, not on a particular place, but some intangible moment in time.

"Do you know what three hundred men trapped for the better part of a day in two oversized floating tin cans smells like? How the July heat cooks you like a can of beans in the fire with a hundred other men? You can't breathe. And you can't go out or they'll shoot you. And all around you is the smell of gunsmoke, the sickly scent of oil as it laps against the barges, the stench of a burning flat car. And all around you men are cryin' and men are wailin'. They don't know what they're doin'—most of 'em would barely know how to hold a gun in the best of times. And this ain't the best of times. There's a man dying slow on the floor, bleeding out from a bullet wound in his arm. At first he was screamin', then moanin', and now he's jus' wimperin', his face white as a sheet and you know it won't be long."

He took a long drag. "And you're just waitin'. And it's just another war and you're tryin' ta figure how you'll get out of this one. Or if you will. Or even if you want to. Cause there'll always be another war. They're shootin' at you from all directions. And you see the face of every man or woman or kid who died at your hand and so you add another to their number and they brand you a murderer for it."

"That sounds like a nightmare," I said.

"Not the worst I've ever had. Coulda been. You know that moment when you face your own mortality?" I nodded. "When the Homesteaders sent a burning flat car down the rail tracks to us, I felt it. As did every other man on those barges."

"Why didn't they jump off?"

"Seems like the reasonable thing to do, right? I'll tell you it was the hardest thing I ever did to resist that urge. Wal, second to burying the only family I had." He shrugged, staring straight ahead as he sucked in another breath full of smoke. "See, the Homesteaders, they had people on the bridge shootin' at us, people on skiffs on the river, jus' waiting for one of us to poke his head out of the metal covering like a prairie dog poking its head out of its hole. They waren't about to let any of us get outta there alive."

"What do you mean?" I was baffled by this. "Would it not have been in their best interests to persuade the Pinkertons to leave and thereby end the fighting?"

"Jus' what I says. We tried to leave, the tug came to get us, American flag streamin' in the wind. They shot at it all the same, until it had to turn around and leave us behind. We tried to surrender, but every time someone would wave the white flag it'd be shot outta their hands."

"What did they mean by that?"

"Simple. They meant to kill us. All of us. Like so many rats." His eyes were staring, but not at me, nor anything else; an unseen fire blazed before them. "Hey, you wanna go see the exposition?" he said, seemingly out of nowhere.

"I suppose so."

"Nah, jus' figured might be good to talk a bit more. But I could use a bit of a walk—stretch my legs a bit. You did want to hear about what happened at Homestead. I'd hate to disappoint a lady such as yourself."

It was so strange to walk on the other side of the street from the broken down houses and factories of the Point. The same gulf seemed just as true from the giant red brick with its shining white trim and gleaming glass and steel as it had on the side of the slums only yards away. I felt I could no more cross over the street to the one than I had been able to the other. The Exposition building was impressive in the way of a Colonial structure, the front facade bringing to mind a modern church, but for the rear of the building which was a rather fascinating structure made almost entirely of steel and glass, reflecting the river and city from its sides.

Tom guided me to a large brick facade trimmed in white molding that stood in slight relief from the front of the building with three large entryways as towering as those of a cathedral. I could not help looking up in awe at the massive portal as we passed through it into a room of bromeliads and blooming exotic flowers. People milled about to the strains of a string quintet.

Booths of every type lined the path, some decorated to match the exotic wares they were selling, others selling popcorn, and still others meant as decorative advertisement. Small garden areas trailed between booths, Parapets, domes and spires rose up, reaching above the second story railings which looked down upon the visitors. It was certainly no Crystal Palace, but it held a charm in its own right.

Tom extended his elbow out toward me and, smiling, I took it in hand. To any passerby we were indistinguishable from a couple enjoying a stroll through the indoor park, our conversation of no consequence to those who might otherwise be tempted to listen.

"Now then, I s'pose I should start at the beginning. Which, I guess, would be when I signed up in Chicago. I saw a poster recruitin' fer a job, didn' say what kind. I said to myself, well any job's better'n starvin' to death. Hadn't held a position since my enlistment expired, ya see. So I signed up. Easy money, got me outta Chicago, seemed like a good deci-sion. Won't say it was the worst of my life, but it's definitely on the list. I shoulda know somethin' was up when they didn' see fit ta tell me even after I had signed my name. But they didn't an' I didn't ask.

"From what the others said when we all got to Bellevue station, ain't none of us were told 'cept that we were gettin' on these two covered barges and we'd be pulled down the river by a tug to our location in the middle of the night to arrive in the mornin'. One of the barges, *Iron Mountain*, was mostly sleepin' quarters—that was the one I was on when it all went to hell. The other had tables and a kitchen with waiters an' everything—that was the Monongahela. Wasn't badly outfitted, neither. They had crates of uniforms and other crates of guns for when we got there. There was a man, Captain Heinde, in charge of the outfit. He was an arrogant sonuva-pardon—sonuva gun. Typical of the type, I guess. It all was goin' fine, but, I don't know, somethin' about the way that deputy spoke to Captain Heinde didn't set right with me. Shrugged it off. Thought Heinde seemed a bit jittery. Honestly, at that point I was jus' thinkin' of the promise of a hot meal served by real waiters. I pitied them the most when it all went bad. All they'd signed up for was to serve food."

"It was real nice. Better food than a lot of us had eaten in months, decent beds. But I still jus' couldn't get over the way Heinde was actin' like he expected somethin' at any moment. I'd seen captains get like that. Saw it at Pine Ridge. Where it's like they know sumpin' you don't and if'n ya did ya prob'ly wouldn't be there with 'em. Kept me from sleeping. Reckon it was good it did. We didn't know what it was or even that it was till we reached what I later was told was the Smithfield Street Bridge. You know, the blue one that looks like a weird pair of eyes starin' at you."

"Yes, I know it."

"Saw some shadows movin' as we approached. Men get up an' start runnin'. Warn't ten minutes later we heard the long whine of a factory whistle. I think a lot of us knew at that moment. Not exactly what was coming—no one there coulda predicted that or we woulda jumped off those barges into the river whether Heinde shot us or not—but you know that sinking feeling you get?"

I nodded. I knew exactly the sensation. The moment you knew a situation was about to fall apart and you would be lucky to escape with your skin.

"Wasn't more'n a few minutes when a little steamer pulled up ahead of us. Seemed a bit strange ta see a steamer so late at night. As it approached, I and a few others saw the men inside pull out rifles. There was scarce enough time to get to cover before they fired on us. Then they blew their whistle, long and high. A moment later, another from somewhere on the shore answered it, though it was too dark to see from where. Then another whistled and another until the whole night air was filled with their howls. And one by one the lights started comin' on on the hillside, like stars poppin' out in the night sky. That was when we saw the worm, long and fiery, start to grow, snaking its way along toward the place we were distressed to find we were headed. Men rushed to the crates to grab guns and uniforms."

He stopped, took out another cigarette and lit it without letting go of my arm. "We hadn't even reached the dock when the first shots were fired from the shore. I heard the sound of breaking glass and bullets like hail on a tin roof as the men from the tugboat, the *Little Bill*, dove for cover. Heinde assured us they had built a fence around the works, that once we were at the bank we'd be safe." He took a long drag on his cigarette. "The Homesteaders went through that fence like it was made of paper."

"It wasn't just workers and men there neither. There were women and kids, and not older kids but these women—some were holdin' a baby in one hand an' a gun in the other. There was even this old lady with a billy club. I remember her cause she gave me this." He pointed to a puffy line of scar flesh above his brow. "Kept screechin' 'bout dirty black sheep. Did worse to some of the others. But that was later."

"They didn't even wait till we had made the wharf afore the whole of the town met us there with muskets and rifles blazing. We fired a few rounds back. Then it all went quiet. But not the good kind. The eerie kind when you know sumpin's gonna happen and you can only wait for it. The *Monongahela* sent out their largest man, big as John Sullivan he was and pacing the deck, starin' at the Homesteaders, darin' them to even try an' shoot him. Then came a shout from the shore, not from a man, but a woman. She was joined in a chorus of heavenly voices spewin' the most ugly and vile things you ever heard. These Homestead angels cussed and cursed, rainin' stones from above at our barges."

He exhaled a plume of smoke. "It was then the crowd got real quiet and that O'Donnell stepped forward. I'll never forget it. Told us the men of Homestead were peaceably inclined. Recommended we send a committee ashore. Given what they had already done, what they would do, who knows what they would have done to a committee? He warned us that whatever we did we must not land or there would be bloodshed. I think most of us on the barges were willing to consider his suggestion. A lot of men were already talkin' how they didn't sign up to be shot at. It was then Captain Heinde stepped out onto the deck of the *Iron Mountain*, the barge I was on, and declared that we were detectives from the Pinkerton Agency and that we had been sent to take possession of the property and guard it. I could tell from a few of the faces hidin' under the beds that this was the first time they were hearin' 'xactly what it was they had signed up for. Then he told them we'd be goin' up there to the works and if they didn't withdraw we would mow every one of them down."

Tom threw his cigarette butt on the path and crushed it with his foot, driving it down until it was merely a spot of pale ash. "Don't know who he expected to mow them down, most of the men were too scared to do anything but cower on the floor of the barge. But it sounded impressive enough to stir the remainder of 'em. Unfortunately, it was a speech better for rallyin' the Homesteaders. Took five men behind O' Donnell to hold 'em back so they wouldn't trample over their leader in their eagerness. Then O'Donnell said, 'I have no more to say. What you do here is at the risk of many lives. Before you enter those mills, you will trample over the dead bodies of three thousand honest working men.' You could see the fires of thousands of lanterns and torches glowing all around us. On both sides of the shore, from the bridges, and in the distance, more fiery worms formed to provide assistance." He paused, then said, "Let's sit for a while." He gestured to a bench and I was glad to have a seat upon it.

He stepped up onto the seat of the bench, setting himself on the edge of the back, like he was sitting on a fence rail. I noticed he was wearing heeled leather boots with something of a squared toe. He took out another cigarette and lit it.

He exhaled heavily. "Captain Heinde gave the order to lower the gangplank. That was when I grabbed a gun from the crate and hid myself behind the wall next to the deck so I could shoot out if the Homesteaders kept their word. Wal, a contingent of 'em, mebbe six in all, approached the gangplank and that was when Heinde told them we were comin' ashore and they couldn't stop us. One of 'em shouted something back like, 'Come on, and you'll come over my carcass!' and threw himself down on the gangplank with his revolver cocked and pointed at Heinde. I'm not sure he'd ever used that thing to shoot a man, but he looked like he'd had enough liquid courage to try. Of course, Captain Heinde didn't care much for his little demonstration and brought his billy club down on the man's head. You could hear shouts from O'Donnell and his men to 'Get back!'—not that it had much effect on the mob."

"Heinde ordered us forward and stepped onto the shore like he was confident three hundred men would follow him. He shoulda watched where he was goin'. Set his foot on an oar and slipped, and the darn thing sprung up and hit some big Slav in the jaw and knocked him out. It would have been a laugh had it not been exactly the wrong time for it to happen."

"I guess they could forgive the strike against the man on the gangplank, but that second one was one too many. A man with a club rushed from the crowd and slammed Heinde with it. Knocked him right off his feet. Couldn't tell you exactly what happened next; there were two shots, and the next thing I knew Heinde and the man on the gangplank were both bleedin'. One of the other captains, Cooper, I think, shouted the order for us to open fire. Might as well have been orderin' the Homesteaders cause they didn't wait for us to start to fire back. I took aim at O'Donnell who had left himself wide open. It was a perfect shot. Clean. Right through the heart."

He pointed his thumb to the center of his chest, spilling ash from his cigarette onto his trousers. "Any kid coulda made it. But just as I was about to shoot, another man knocked my arm an' I only grazed his thumb." He spat behind us. "A man went down in front of me, I pulled him in, bleedin' badly as he was. I fired a few more rounds into the crowd. Hard to say what missed and what hit in that mess."

"In less'n ten minutes it was over. At least a dozen Homesteaders were lyin' on the shore, some dead, some dying. You could hear their cries from the barge. On our side weren't much different. I counted at least a dozen shot, probably more, not counting Captain Heinde who had clawed his way over the gangplank where one of the officers yanked him back on deck by the seat of his pants. Some of the Pinkerton commanders wanted to launch another assault, but Potter, the good superintendent, wouldn't hear of having more blood on his hands without the sheriff's go ahead. So there we sat, waiting, while the Homesteaders carried away their wounded and dead behind a makeshift barricade of iron. A few of the men on the barge asked Potter if we might head back from where we came, but he assured them that it looked like the Advisory Committee had the crowd under control and soon negotiations could take place. I guess he really believed that, because he sent the tug away with Captain Heinde and the other wounded."

"Course I wasn't about ta believe that anymore'n the others were. We could hear clear as day those Homesteaders callin' to 'Kill the Pinkertons.' I took out my knife an started cuttin' a window into the side of the barge. If they were gonna shoot me, I wanted to at least be able ta give 'em a fight. A number of the other men, the ones not hidin' under their beds, did the same. I saw O'Donnell directin' the women to leave; they weren't too keen on the idea but they did go. That was when I knew it was time to reload my Winchester."

"He was conferrin' with a couple'a other men—they were directin' the others about in a way that was none too encouraging. Settin' up fortifications and the like. Didn't matter what Potter said, it was clear to every man on that barge that there wasn't gonna be any negotiations.

And there we were, floatin' in a tin can on the shore, no way out. Jest waitin'." Tom dropped his cigarette to the ground and lit a third.

"I suppose they decided the best thing they could do was make short work of us before we could get reinforcements. I caught the words 'national guard' a few times. They surrounded our barges with skiffs, shootin' at any man who so much as showed a toe out of cover. After a few hours, one of our captains decided to make another go of it and made his intentions known to the Homesteaders. Wal, you can imagine how that went over. Words were hardly out of his mouth before they began shooting. We fired back. It was then I heard the cannon from the other side of the river boom for the first time. The ball tore right through the metal covers—might as well have been made of tin foil for all the good they did."

"That was when panic set in on the barges. Men went crazed. Took everything jus' to keep 'em from jumpin' into the river where the men on skiffs were waiting. The shootin' began at eight and didn't really stop after that. Minutes jus' passin' by one after another, turning to hours and hours. Moanin' from the wounded. Death all around us. Watched a cannonball strike the works, saw it send a piece of iron right through a man's head. It was enough to make even the sanest man start to lose his mind." He was staring at one of the booths, but his gaze never fell upon it. The cigarette between his fingers slowly turned to ash and wilted.

"What did you do?" I asked, almost afraid to know his part.

"Ah slept."

"You what?" I was astonished; I could not have heard him right.

"I'd been up since Chicago, I was tired. Nothin' was changin' anytime soon, so I jest set myself down and had a nap. Wasn't like they wouldn't wake me if somethin' happened."

What sort of man could consider a hail of bullets a suitable lullaby? I marveled to myself.

He continued the tale, telling how the tug returned for them, how it had fled in a hail of bullets before reaching them. How the sight of its flag vanishing in the distance left the men on the barges devastated. About their hysteria as they watched the Homesteaders fill a raft with lumber and set it alight, drifting toward the barges with the intent to set them aflame as was once done to the Spanish fleet in the British Channel. This had proved unsuccessful, as had a second attempt to send a flaming flat car into the barges, which had only managed to roll as far as the water's edge before stopping.

He told how the captains threatened to shoot anyone who jumped from the barges into the water. The attempts by the Homesteaders to dynamite the barges. Of the Homesteaders pouring oil into the river with the intent to set it on fire. How the hail of bullets never ceased. How one of those bullets hit a man who had been cowering under cover with his head in his hands. He described the moans and cries of agony as the man slowly bled to death on the floor of the barge, the red liquid life flowing onto the floor, sticking to their shoes. How this had finally convinced the others on the barge to formally surrender, and how their white flags had been shot from their hands when they tried.

"They refused to allow you to surrender?" I asked.

He nodded.

"Why?"

"Reckon they wanted us dead before the authorities could intervene."

"But three hundred men!"

"Wouldn't've made a difference if we were three thousand men. We killed seven of 'em and they were going to make each one of us pay for 'em as if we had shot 'em personally. Which, consequently, I had."

"You did mention that."

"His name was John Morris. He had a wife and kids."

"You know his name?"

"I know 'em all, even the ones we didn't kill that died because of us. I'm so tired of killing."

"I understand."

He lit the cigarette. "We can't change what we've done. Only live with it, I guess."

"I suppose so. What happened then? As you are still alive, I can assume they did eventually allow your surrender."

"A man came from the national office of the union. He called for them to let us go. Worked about as well as those white flags. Then O'Donnell appeared on top of a pile of steel beams holding a giant American flag like he was some sort of paragon of the working man and commanded silence. The Homesteaders claim O'Donnell wasn't the leader of the mob, but I'll tell you, if you had seen how they cheered him when he appeared, how they even took their hats off jest to hear him speak, you wouldn't wonder that he was. Well the short of it is, they agreed to let us off the barges, so long as we were surrendered to their custody until the sheriff could come get us. Under the condition we would be tried for murder." He threw his cigarette on the ground, only half smoked. "He assured us that if we surrendered under those conditions, we would not be harmed."

"Our captains objected, but we could not bear to wait for our deaths like so many rats any longer. Again we raised the white flag and this time they allowed us to surrender. I wish I could say that was the end of it, but as bad as everything had been up until this point, it somehow managed to get even worse. The walk to the opera house was probably the longest walk of my life. It was clear O' Donnell's words were worth less than the time it took to speak 'em."

"They led us out from the barges with a man taking charge of each of us, like we was prisoners. I remember the moment I emerged from the barge, hands up. A man grabbed me roughly by the arm and yanked me down the gang plank so hard I fell in the water to the hoots and jeers of the crowd. That was when a rock got me above the eye. Couldn't see much after that on account of the blood on one side." He rubbed his thumbnail across a mostly healed cut over his brow.

"The man pulled me out of the water and threw me before the crowd. Fists flew at me from every angle. I felt sticks and clubs as I was pulled through the crush of people all doing their very best to get in their blows for my crime. I couldn't see anything but hands and bodies and clubs. Jest had to follow where I was being pulled by a man I could scarcely see."

He rolled another cigarette and lit it, taking a long drag. "I felt rocks pelting me from behind, bouncing off my coat and hat. I tripped over another detective who was lying curled on the ground. There was only a bloody hole where his eye had been. A man, much like the one dragging me, was jeering at him, trying to get a hold of his arm to pull him back up, but the detective clamped them to his side even as a barrage of kicks assaulted him from every angle. They flew at me as well, striking me in the side, the face, hard boots, pointed lady's shoes, even bare feet. My guard jerked me to my feet and continued to pull me through the gauntlet. I remember taking a hard blow to the gut that nearly knocked me off my feet, but I held my ground and kept going."

"We emerged through the gate of the steelworks into the town and then our miseries truly began. We were set upon by the townspeople with all the fury of wolves starvin' for blood. I remember we reached a building that I later found out was union headquarters, the Bost building, an' the man guiding me stopped, punched me in the gut and told me to remove my hat and salute the flag. I couldn't even see the flag, but I reached for my hat. Wasn't fast enough for his liking and he tore it from my head and threw it on the ground, then pointed and shouted 'salute!' so I did as best I could and he laughed and jerked me along. I stopped even bein' able to feel the pain anymore, just the dull thud of unceasing blows. I can't tell you the relief I felt when I was finally thrown through the doors of the opera house and the blows finally ceased. I landed amongst a pile of men, some of whom I recognized from the *Iron Mountain*, some I didn't—some I couldn't for how badly beaten they were. But we were safe. Until the Homesteaders started tryin' to get in that is."

"The man next to me told me 'This is it. They're going to kill us.' And I don't believe he was wrong. Had they been allowed in they would have probably torn us limb from limb eventually. That was when the guards finally decided we'd had enough and threatened to shoot the next person who came at us, pitiful bloodied creatures that we were. Eventually, all of us were in and that was where we stayed with nary a nurse to tend our wounds until Sheriff McCleary arrived at midnight to escort us by train to the county jail. At least, so we thought."

"That was when Frank saw me—he was on the train waiting to receive us. The Pinkerton Agency sent him to evaluate the situation. I was a sorry sight by any measure, but he recognized me. Asked how would I like to join him in the investigation. 'Anything ta keep my head outta the noose,' I says. When the train stopped at the station, he smuggled me off. From what I heard the rest of the men were secreted away in the middle of the night. Don't know what became of most of 'em. A few filed claims against the Pinkertons sayin' if they'd known what they were in for they wouldn't've signed up. The agency contacted Frick about it and he just told them it was their own fault and none of his responsibility that we weren't told. I wouldn't mind popping Frick one in the face, myself, after what he put us through."

"I can't say that I blame you."

He stood up and extended a hand to me. "It's gettin' rather late in the mornin'. What's say we get some popcorn and then send you on the train back."

I nodded and took his hand. "That sounds a fine idea," I said, squashing the pile of cigarette butts and ash under my shoe as I followed his lead.

Life Work
An Interview with Larry Smith, Author and Publisher

Larry Smith, Professor Emeritus, Bowling Green State University's Firelands College in Huron, Ohio, is the author of nine books of poetry, eight books of fiction, and two literary biographies. He has been the editor-publisher of Bottom Dog Press for 35 years. In that time, his commitment to the literature of the working class in all its diversity has led him to publish some of the most significant contemporary works to come out of the Appalachian region. As author Timothy Dodd has said of Smith, "He's a marvel, in his output and what he's accomplished for our region, history, and spirit."

EP: Your latest book of poems is *The Pears*, and your earliest collection, *Across These States, A Journal* appeared back in 1985. How do these collections reflect your life?

LS: *Across These States* was a journal poem, the first book Bottom Dog Press did. I traveled across the United States by Amtrak and back in 1984, going out West to interview people about the San Francisco Renaissance. That wasn't long after my father had passed away, so my head was full of thoughts and feelings. It's a journal of what's going on in the train and outside the train as I journeyed across the United States to California.

You know sometimes when you get older you feel like you're done writing? I thought my imagination was getting further away from me, but those poems in *The Pears*—maybe it was some reading I was doing of younger poets or going back to those surrealist roots I had—I just let my imagination go and wrote something like dream poems. The quote inside the book is from Charles Simic, "When they ask for apples, give them pears." Don't do what's expected. Do what surprises you in some way. I studied surrealism in a National Endowment for the Humanities seminar at Syracuse University, and it stayed with me. I wouldn't say I'm a surrealist poet, but I am interested in automatic writing and trusting the irrational. That's always been in my poems. Even though much of my writing is very "down home," going back to my mill town roots, the imagination is still there. The thing about surrealistic writing is a real trust that you can communicate irrationally—and measure success as when someone gets it.

After fifty years of writing, I see myself going back to go forward. I recently finished a book of poems called *Mingo Town*. My hometown is Mingo Junction, Ohio; and I had recently read another writer's novel centered in Youngstown. She, Susan Petrone, lets Youngstown speak. Youngstown talks to us in her book. So, I thought, "What would Mingo Junction say to me?" and wrote a series of monologues of Mingo speaking. They're prose poems—"Mingo Dreaming," "Mingo Speaking History," "Mingo Out Walking." They took me back to those roots: Appalachia, the steel mills, working-class neighborhoods.

EP: Why prose poems?

LS: I've been sharing those poems with people from Mingo Junction, and I think they're more accessible as prose than as poetry. And Mingo just talks in prose; that's all I can say. It talks in slang a little. It talks the way people down home talk, bold and direct sometimes, and yes, in images and metaphors, too. It was fun. It was really great to release that town in me in stories.

EP: How has Mingo Junction changed over the years? Is it typical of Appalachian towns?

LS: Mingo has shrunk by about one-third. It's a steel mill town and yet the steel mills are gone. Economically, it's depressed; but there are good people there, people caring for each other. Where the town or state can't afford to clean the streets or pave the park, they're doing it. We go back home because we still have family there, so I'm pleased to find that people still care. But downtown, some of the buildings have caved in, and the storefronts are dark. It's not a pretty town anymore, and yet people are nostalgic about it. I don't want to write so that people feel sorry for it, though, because it has character. That comes out in my book when Mingo speaks.

EP: Did you start writing poetry when you lived in Mingo Junction?

LS: I started writing in the sixth grade. My sixth-grade English teacher would pass out these little Haldeman-Julius poems. They were published real cheaply, those Haldeman-Julius booklets. She would give them to us and say, "These are for you. These are yours now." We would read the poems on Friday, and she would ask us to write our own poems and read them out loud the next Friday. She set expectations, and her valuing the language in that way inspired me and others. At Muskingum College, I started as a math major because that was during the Sputnik era when science and math were so valued. But in college I found my way to literature; and I thought, "Man, I could get paid to read these books and talk about them! That's the career for me."

EP: Whose work do you love that's not by one of the authors you've published?

LS: Actually, I've gone back, and I read Thoreau all the time. His writing is so sane and so meaningful, especially now. And last year I got into Melville and *Moby Dick*. I've read that book five times, but I really got into it, appreciating it in a deeper way. Then most recently I'm rereading Albert Camus' *The Plague*. It helps in getting through this pandemic. He never lived through a plague, but it's so parallel to what we're going through, even predicting the behavior and changes in the attitudes. It's a book that has deep meaning for me.

EP: You've published books by members of the Southern Appalachian Writers Collaborative (SAWC). What does the work of these writers tell you about similarities between northern and southern Appalachia? Differences?

LS: We're a little more urban in northern Appalachia. I've published writers from both areas. . . . I've lived mostly in northern Appalachia, and published writers from northern Appalachia. I sense that we're more ethnically diverse in character. Bottom Dog published *Portrait of the Artist as a Bingo Worker* by Lori Jakiela, about her growing up in a Polish American family and working in a Bingo parlor with her grandma. The stories are different because place is so important.

EP: You've published some books of your own and by others that embrace Zen writings. How does this Asian connection fit into your life?

LS: We all have a spiritual journey we're on. I love the writings of Gary Snyder, Jack Kerouac, and other dharma bums also: Lawrence Ferlinghetti, the Beat writers, Kenneth Patchen. I think it was just my own self-discovery and spiritual journey that brought me to that. I wrote an article once called "Working-Class Zen." I talked in it about my railroader father; the things he taught me were very much like Zen, very practical—things like "Let the shovel do its work." My wife Ann's grandmother, an Italian woman who didn't go beyond first grade, was a wise person. She had a real humble spiritual aura about her, yet she was practical. So, I connected to that sense of it. Also, I went to a Presbyterian school. In later years, I joined the Catholic Church. I didn't believe in everything the church says, but I believed in a lot of it, and felt there was so much value there and depth. I'm still a Buddhist. I don't know what you'd call me . . . a Christian-Buddhist, I guess; but I try to stay open to all others. I meditate for health and sanity, to ground myself, to lose that "monkey mind" that gets caught up with tweets and the media. Buddhism's affected my writing. I've done a few books centered on it, and Ray McNiece and I did *American Zen*, an anthology, with poets from around the country.

EP: You did a book of translations, didn't you, with another writer?

LS: Mei Hui Lui, from Taiwan. She was my student, and we ended up teaching each other, you know? I was teaching her how to do English a little better. We were sharing poetry by Chinese Zen writers, and then we did two books of translations. Those books still sell. We go to Appalachian conferences, and people end up buying Zen poetry. I think there's a connection.

EP: What was your translation process?

LS: I don't speak or read Chinese. I read translations, the great body of translations we have. We would agree on a poem, and Mei would find it in its original and translate the Chinese characters to English and give it to me. I would try to make it American English and give it back to her, and she would make her changes. Thanks to emails we were able to do that, as she moved back to Taiwan eventually. It was a slow process, but we weren't in a hurry. We tried to stay very close to the Chinese. When we published the last book of Ryokan's, it was English and Chinese and Japanese, so people could read it in any or all of those.

You were asking about the influence of Zen: it's basic and direct and it's real, and that's kind of Appalachian. Both writings avoid the flowery to keep in touch with the life flow.

EP: I notice that one of Bottom Dog's recent books is entitled *I Reckon: Haiku and Haibun*. It's part of your Laurence Dunbar Series.

LS: Francis Alexander Sandusky showed up at our coffeehouse readings, and I found out that he's published in all kinds of haiku magazines. Haibun, you know, is writing prose—a journal—and then you drop in a haiku, then a prose poem, and then another haiku.

EP: I don't know another small press that has accomplished as much as Bottom Dog Press has. What do you want to get done in the coming years?

LS: Since retiring, I'm home and have more time. We've done three books of poetry in half a year. So, I plan to continue to meet that mission of publishing for underserved audiences. Appalachia is a place where people actually do read and do care about literature, so it's great that we have that series, and we have the Working Lives series. Those stories matter. Like Haldeman-Julius publishing those cheap books for people, not for libraries, not hard-bound copies to go up on shelves: we make good writing available and treat place and people with respect and dignity.

Grave Blankets

You have to love the local grocer,
Who sells fresh produce and grave blankets

Glistening under the misting sprinklers
And evergreen in the window.

The whole life cycle,
Marked down from yesterday's prices.

Business Decisions

Grandma's policy toward snakes was chopping them
into pieces first and naming later.
Moving to town didn't tame her—that's how
the garter snake died under the sharp hoof
of her hoe, its "business end" we say (no chicken house
but the patio was saved). Little snake parts writhed
like sausages sizzling on her slate.

She and Grandpa got hard things done, like selling
the Childers Run farm to a man who ran coal. That
changed my mom's childhood memories to cash.
When she drove there to dream one evening it was
crawling with dozers, that homestead she'd thought
to own: land when Grandpa'd made that Cutright man,
when he signed the deed, promise not to strip.

What Suits, You?

late October 2020

The plaid flannel of the boy next door
says "Millennial," along with the beard
and the old briar pipe. Signs of the times.

So what to make of the suits
in Washington, their narrow
palettes of blues and grays,
their fat bright ties
like front windows in Las Vegas?
And what about their aides and secretaries,
their strangling conservative ensembles,
their tight-waisted monochrome numbers
with the poopsie labels "Kailey"
or "Kellyanne"?

Never once have I seen
in foreground or background
on TV from the Capitol
a man in a stained t-shirt and bluejeans,
hair slicked back, a pack of Luckies
rolled into his shirt sleeves,
pushing a necessary broom.

He's my kind of guy, fellow citizen,
someone out of Steubenville
in the 1950s, his dad an old buddy of Dino's,
his slick uncle Guido
transparently, straightforwardly mean,

worthy of interview at least—
an equal access felon,
much better spoken than any high-end crook
that we have ever seen,
President Company included.

The Gift of Guitar

She strums; the river runs.
Her fingers sway like poplar trees
    branches waving in the breeze, swept with sunlight
    brushing low against the banks of
    wide rolling waters.
She strums; the river runs
    tripping skipping in silvery streams
down steel strings.
We muse at the music.
    We wade, ankles wet, through the sound of our own
    sorrow, serenity, silent prayer.
    Some deep internal part is drawn—
                    to be drawn . . .
                            slowly lifted and drawn
                    drawn and sifted
            as silt in the current
    washed and moved
            cleansed and carried with the river.
She holds back
        her hand;
the river sleeps.
Fingers flutter forward; the river weeps.
    A catfish sweeps its lengthy tail, grins sagely
    flurries away like a dream upon waking.
She strums; the river runs.

Slag

"Isn't this one pretty? Keep it," commanded Donna Sue, my friend and compatriot in public service.

She thrust at me a sharp-edged and irregular piece of historic trash plucked from the daisies in our national forest. Neither the park's historian nor conservationist made a peep as Donna Sue gave away this shimmering relic, irrevocably separating it from the iron furnace decomposing to our left.

Obsidian green and vaguely translucent, the slag was heavier than it looked. This hunk of industrial refuse had lain in the tall grass for more than a hundred years, left behind by countless workers, then campers and hunters.

I obediently put the baseball-sized chunk on the floorboards of my car, for one does not question Donna Sue (who has the mystical authority of a mountain witch, complete with Birkenstocks and a broomstick skirt).

The cold, silent furnace didn't object, either. I half expected her to raise her weed-covered mound and cry out, "Kidnappers!" as I carted off the bastard child once belched from her belly. The slag was irreplaceable; begot by long dead, anonymous men in a smelting process forgotten in time. There would be no more.

In the following weeks, I took the slag home, to work, and everywhere else I drove in that car, forgetting all about the relic, occasionally hearing it clunk, and covering it up with twentieth-century trash until I was clearing out the car one day, and a jagged edge cut me. So, I sucked on my finger and tossed the chunk into a flower bed with stones my then-toddler, Dom, collected. We called this space the Treasure Bed and created it so my son wouldn't fill his room with rocks, sticks, pinecones and leaves. Then, I promptly forgot about the slag, again.

Eventually, Dom brought it to me and asked what it was. So, we sat down on all the common rocks he usually held in high esteem to examine the interloper. In that moment, the slag transformed like a dancer hitting her rhythm for the first time. It became more than it was because I saw it through his eyes.

Holding it up to the sunlight, Dom and I closely inspected the transitions of color (midnight green and opal black) as the shades rolled over each other like a frozen wave in the ocean. We savored its smooth planes and bladed jags. We peered through it as if it were a kaleidoscope until we found the springy greens suspended in its depths. It was reborn, not as trash, but treasure.

For months, Dom packed it around in his chubby little hands, set it near him when he played, and placed it in the Treasure Bed by the door so it couldn't get lost. Holding it to the sun would cheer him with a consistency previously reserved for new race cars and magic bubble wands, pulling him forcibly from the land of introverts to a present reality, firing our imaginations with green flames.

But that was before I saw that everyday mysticism was the center of life (or at least before I accepted it).

I didn't take the black-green slag from the flowerbed when we moved away in a frantic, exhausted, overworked rush. No one pointed out the slag's irreplaceable nature or threw it on the floorboards as the moving van pulled away. If only the slag itself could have risen up from among its limestone, pebble, and pine-twig neighbors to scream, "Forgotten!"

Sometimes I wonder, all these years later, if the kids in the new family found our treasure and became connoisseurs of its opaque glory. Or maybe, they just ignored the weird rock. I wonder if some old timer wandered by, knew the piece was furnace slag, and wondered how the hell that trash got there with no iron works for miles and miles.

Even though I drive by our old house sometimes, I'm not brave enough to stop and ask. Because what if this gift from the furnace, from my friend, and from my son is just gone? What if it has been consigned to oblivion by my failure to respect its unique glory?

I left it to lie alone in the grass for another hundred years until someone sees its potential.

Perhaps the next person will mistake it for cosmic garbage flung here from another planet. Perhaps she will imagine a world where men of superhuman strength toiled endlessly, until their backs broke and their lungs turned black. Perhaps she will conjure great steaming monsters on clanking wheels that carried creations from a fiery furnace to faraway places. Perhaps she will know that iron born of violent wombs once became the bones of gleaming highrises that pierced soot-filled, gray-green skies.

PLACE

Tonight, There Is the Moon

Someone builds a fire, hot dogs
sizzle, crisp to popping point.
Succulence abounds in simplicity
as evening crawls up the ridge,
cushions us in dusk-soft insect chatter.

Before earth tilts forward
to see Buck Moon,
wide meadow dances with fireflies.
This land breathes all its tiny lives.

Anxious for lunar eclipse,
we gaze upward, when suddenly
a whip-poor-will serenade
lifts like a blessing.

Predictable as evolution,
coyotes begin to howl. The pack,
in full vibrato, echoes a shiver
into our ears, as mice
and possum scurry for cover.

Do you know everything
is made of like matter?
Oxygen, hydrogen, carbon, nitrogen,
universal stardust.

Tonight, the moon shows full.

Following Spirit

I work a puzzle at the table.
A pastoral, rural scene.
The cupola of a barn.
The knob of a shed door.
All pieces of the whole.
A sawhorse in the yard.
The serrated teeth of our words.
I work remotely now.
Where the spirit flies memory follows.
What does it mean—jig before saw—
and jigsaw before puzzle?
What exactly is spirit?—
The ridge of a cliff?—
The transparent birds
flying over the sharp line of trees?
I see straight through their bodies
where other worlds live.
I am putting the parts together—
a rung of the moon—
the sun rocking back and forth in the sky.

Moundsville Trains

My mother loses her confidence on Rankin's Turn up the steep grade.
Traffic blocked, her clutch foot burns and stalls the Mustang.
She had driven us to the library, past cold Fostoria stacks,
The card catalog of family businesses dying down Jefferson.
I must be six and unbuckled, my sister bundled in her car seat.
Horns chorus, and the smoke lifts blue and stinging as tears.
A man knocks on the window, and she leaves us to him, watches
From the median, a bright blouse on a drear hillside. He gives no
    name,
Drives us to the top. With the grunt of the parking brake, he meets
    my eye
In the rear view: *deal with it*. And I chew boldly on my book.
The memories set in glass and metalwork, the stink of the river,
The Adena burial mound, shadows of churches, Mitchell plant sky.
The drivers of Moundsville stream by more determined than ever,
Long black trains coughing from every open window, every word
    they mouth.

Running Numbers for Chocolate

Late one summer afternoon when I was six, I was playing alone in front of Mr. Corazza's grocery store on the ground floor of our building on Larimer Avenue. I wasn't allowed to venture beyond my block unless my mother walked me to Grandma's house two blocks away or to play with one of my friends on Lenora Street. I didn't mind playing in front of our building. It was my place in the neighborhood, where I belonged.

I was on threezies in a game of jacks when one of the neighborhood men called to me. "Linda, come here," beckoned Mr. Galiano, waving.

That's the day it began—my chocolate gig.

Mr. Galiano was a fixture on our block, spending most days with a small group of men sitting on the stoop in front of Mrs. Gentilcore's chicken store a few doors away. He was stocky with a bald head and a round face, made larger by a mass of chewing tobacco tucked in his cheek. In the summer, Mr. Galiano usually wore a straw hat with a black grosgrain band. Neighborhood men and women would stop by to hand him small pieces of paper that he would slip into the hat band.

There were three types of men in our neighborhood: working men like my dad, shopkeepers like Mr. Corazza, and small-time criminals. Everyone coexisted, sharing the taverns, shops, neighborhood streets, and the church, which seemed to resemble organized crime in some ways—both rigidly hierarchical with established guidelines, similar vows of silence, and unquestioned power. In our neighborhood, it was okay to violate the law, but not your family, or the church, or the Wize guys.

Larimer Avenue was my mother's neighborhood. She was born and raised there. While it would be years before anyone in my mom's family became involved in petty criminal activity, she was a neighborhood girl, enculturated from birth into the ways of this place. She understood the roles adopted by each type of neighbor; she recognized where power resided; she knew how things worked—all lessons that I would come to learn as well. When I was a young adult, Mom told me that she had dated an underboss for one of the big five crime families. "We were young at the time," she explained, "before he moved up from soldier to underboss." I thought it exciting that a mob boss could have been my father. I could have been a mafia princess, showered with diamond bracelets, vacations to Rome, maybe my own Alpha Romeo. Organized crime translated to wealth and freedom from hard work. Of course, Mom had also dated the huckster.

Criminal activity didn't seem unusual in my family. My favorite uncle was a dealer in a private club run by the Italian mob. When I was old enough, he shared with me that he had attended the infamous 1957 Apalachin, New York, Meeting where he dealt cards for the one hundred or so Mafioso bosses who met there. Uncle told the story with some degree of pride. My mom's oldest sister ran a numbers book out of her small apartment in a public housing high rise. Her oldest son was her numbers boss. For us, small-time crime was part of the norm, an accepted fact of life for the working poor.

My dad on the other hand was an outsider who moved to Larimer Avenue when he married Mom. He wasn't a neighborhood boy, but he became acquainted with the guys who sat on the stoop. Dad liked to play the numbers. On the Saturday after pay day, he, too, would stop in front of the chicken store and drop off his folded piece of paper along with a one-dollar bill.

Dad had a system for selecting which number he'd play. It involved methodically recording the numbers that hit each day in a little brown vinyl-covered notebook. Dad would study the numbers, the frequency, and the order in which they came out, in an attempt to calculate the odds. This, mind you, without a computer or even a calculator. Dad also consulted a tattered paper "dream book" where he would look up dreams to determine their meaning, not in the Freudian sense, but to correlate the dream to a three-digit number. Dad would thumb through the yellowed pages of the dream book. Dreamed of frying zucchini flowers? Play 638. Dreamed you were sneezing? Play 712 for one sneeze, 529 if you sneezed twice, and 483 if you sneezed three times. While I overheard conversations between my dad and uncle about playing the numbers—which number to play, whether it was best to play it straight or boxed, and so on—I didn't really understand how it all worked or who was involved. And I certainly didn't know that the numbers game was illegal.

I walked toward Mr. Galiano past the baskets of tomatoes and peaches that lined the front of the grocery and past Henry Grasso's store where links of plump sausages hung in the window.

As I approached, Mr. Galiano pulled the little pieces of folded paper from his hat band. "Here," he said in a raspy voice, "take these across the street to the candy store and they'll give you a chocolate bar."

It seemed a peculiar request, but the chocolate bar piqued my interest, and the storefront had always appeared empty, so I was curious to see inside. "I'm not allowed to cross the street," I replied.

Mr. Galiano and his friends howled with laughter. "Come on; I'll cross you."

I stuffed my jacks in one pocket of my shorts and the tiny pink rubber ball in the other. Mr. Galliano placed the folded papers in my small hand and closed my fingers carefully around them. Then, he walked me to the curb and looked each way.

"All clear," he said. "Go ahead and cross."

Larimer Avenue was the commercial center of our neighborhood, busy with cars and shoppers and lined with stores selling groceries, hardware, and household goods, Conte's drug store, Ursula's beer store, and a gas station on the corner by the Larimer Bridge. I had never been on the other side of Larimer Avenue without my mother. We always crossed together, whether we were on our way to my grandmother's house two blocks away, or when we went to Ursula's beer store across from our apartment to say hello to my mother's long-time friend. Now, here I was crossing the street by myself, and I knew my mother wouldn't approve.

I ran across the street and onto the pavement. As I reached for the door handle of the candy store, I noticed grime on the door and on the glass storefront windows. I left the sunlit street outside and entered the dimly lit store. The large room seemed strangely empty with only one candy case—also with dirty glass—in the center. I studied the options in the case: Clark Bar, Baby Ruth, Oh Henry. My favorite, Mounds Bar, was nowhere in sight. Nothing could compare to the rich dark chocolate and coconut filling of a Mounds Bar. As I stared at the disappointing selection, someone approached through a door in the back of the store.

"Well, young lady, what brings you here?"

I looked up at a tall man with thick dark hair and a greying moustache. Immaculately dressed in a crisp white shirt, it occurred to me that he was the only thing in the store that was clean. I felt intimidated by his presence. He was someone I didn't know—a stranger to me in my neighborhood. His dress, neatly trimmed moustache, and the way he carried himself with poise told me he wasn't one of the guys from the stoop. "I have pieces of paper," I stammered, "and Mr. Galiano said I could get a chocolate bar."

The man threw his head back, laughing. "Well, come with me," he said and opened the door to reveal a back room. "You don't want that stale candy. I have some in the back."

The small back room held a desk littered with papers and a few men sitting around on wooden chairs. "We have a delivery," said the dark-haired man, smiling as he took the folded papers from my hands. He passed them to a portly man with thinning hair and glasses sprawled in a chair behind the desk. Then he reached on a shelf and pulled down several boxes containing chocolate bars. As soon as I saw the dark brown carton with the familiar lettering, I knew I hit pay dirt.

Each afternoon, I'd walk to the chicken store and Mr. Galiano would hand me the small papers from his hat band and watch while I crossed the street. I'd deliver the papers to the tall man with the moustache in return for a Mounds Bar. It was perfection.

I had been delivering the papers in exchange for chocolate bars for several days when late one afternoon I climbed the steps to our second-floor apartment in time for dinner. As I walked in the door, I smelled the aroma of home-fried potatoes. My mom turned from the stove when she heard me come in. "I've been waiting for you." Then, she looked at me closely. "Where did you get chocolate?" I realized that I must not have wiped my mouth. I didn't respond, and she asked again. "Linda, where did you get chocolate?"

Even at six years old, I knew not to test my mother. So, I told her the whole story.

Her face stiffened. "Get cleaned up for dinner," she said quietly.

I had no sooner washed my face and hands at the kitchen sink, when my dad came in. Dad worked as a laborer for the City of Pittsburgh's parks department. He left each morning, lunch pail in hand, and took the streetcar to Mellon Park in Shadyside. After a day of tending to park trails, trimming hedges, and maintaining equipment, Dad returned tired and hungry. His arrival meant that it was time for dinner, and within minutes we were sitting at the kitchen table.

I'm not sure what motivated my mom to tell Dad about the chocolate. "Guess what Linda did today?" Out poured every detail. Dad put down his fork, straightened in his chair, and stared at me. His hazel eyes met mine, but his face lacked expression, and I couldn't tell what he was thinking.

My dad was over six feet tall with muscular arms and broad shoulders, yet he generally spoke softly and sparingly, even when he was angry. Once, some years later when my little sister fell and hit her head on the corner of a marble topped coffee table, my dad, silent and calm, picked up the table right there in the living room and methodically broke off each leg one at a time while my mother watched in horror. She loved that table. But Dad had warned many times that a marble top with sharp edges was not safe around a toddler.

I had never been on the wrong end of my father's anger, so I braced myself for what might come. I wasn't afraid of him—Dad had never raised his hand or his voice to me—but I was worried that I might have somehow disappointed him. He got up from his chair, went to the door, and left the apartment without a word. My mom went after him. "Just let it be," she cried out. "It won't happen again. Dan, please!" I had no idea where my dad was going or why mom was so upset. I felt a bit uneasy that my eating chocolate before dinner had caused such an upheaval.

Mom returned to the kitchen alone, and she and I sat at the table without eating or talking. We waited. Mom fidgeted in her chair, repeatedly glancing over her shoulder toward the door. I sat still, staring at Mom.

After what seemed like hours, but was likely minutes, Dad walked through the door. He sat in his chair and picked up his fork. He took a few bites of cold potatoes then turned to me. "It's over," he said, and I knew that he meant my chocolate gig. We never spoke of it again. After that day, Mr. Galiano didn't call to me. He seemed to avoid even looking at me when I played on the sidewalk close to the chicken store. Sometimes, I'd see him leave the stoop and walk across the street. I envied him and wondered if he would get a candy bar.

I thought about all of this years later the first time that I saw the film "A Bronx Tale" and recognized my dad in DeNiro's character of Lorenzo, the bus driver. Lorenzo, the working man trying to protect his child from the criminal element that pervaded his neighborhood. Lorenzo, who told his son that the men on the street corner were not tough, that the working man was the real tough guy. My dad was Lorenzo.

As a six-year-old, my brief stint running numbers caused me to make some observations about my neighborhood. I noticed how the men who sat on the stoop and who sometimes stood on the sidewalk in front of the candy store disappeared inside when a police car drove down Larimer Avenue. I wondered what they might have to hide. I also noticed a distinction between the working men who left home early each morning on a streetcar and those who didn't seem to ever go to work. I came to realize that my dad and men like Mr. Galiano were different. While I began to understand the roles that people in my neighborhood played, I wasn't yet clear of my own role. I navigated between temptation and guilt, knowing about—and sometimes wanting—the easy rewards that presented themselves, but not always willing to do what it took to reap them. As I grew older, I began to carve out my own place in the neighborhood, ultimately leaning away from the stoop guys, bending toward the values and loving protection of my dad.

Mountains

They were never snow-capped or alone
as the Kilimanjaro on my Hemingway
paperback flap.

They were mostly trees. Their leaves were good
as night for making you feel untouched. Just
the occasional gunshot crack reminded you
of other lives, schoolmates
hunting 12-point bucks. Like quilts

we shoved aside on our beds, they were humped
and unkempt, frustrating
Masterminds who wanted them smooth
as a businessman's hands
and patted our backs. But we knew the world

wasn't flat. To us it was more like a fortress
where baron castles
crowned the ridge, where we hung
our houses and carved gardens
as hickory fumed the peaks
we named *Horsepen, Backbone* and *Cheat*. Cresting

those vistas on road trips, you saw how vast they really were,
like the sea you were desperate to reach.

Topping Trees in Woodsdale

The tree stands, bare branches raised to heaven,
as I turn the corner to Echo Lane.
Its image has gone viral: naked limbs
featured in the social media campaign

waged by my neighbor, the Ent Wife, who lives
one block over on Poplar Street. Her job of
extension agent has her roaming the county,
working with farmers, but her first love

is trees. A week has passed since the chainsaw,
the wood chipper, the dump truck blocked the street,
surrounded the tree and hacked until it
became a dying sculpture, the sole tree

with no buds, no blooms this Lenten season,
and Easter just days away. A thin rim
of dark brown mulch encircles the tree's roots,
but my neighbor has shaken her head, grim

in her pronouncement that resurrection
is not possible. In two years, or one,
chainsaws will return, the trunk will be razed,
stump ground: all reduced to oblivion.

She lives on Poplar; I live on Maple.
Woodsdale: a name for trees in a valley,
a history of streets, houses, creeks, yards,
alleys, bicycles, dogs, children, family.

Will it matter one day if there is Maple
with no maples, Poplar with no poplars,
Walnut with no walnuts, Pine with no pines?
Mountains with no tops and only hollers?

The tree confronts me on my daily walks.
I see its stark, knotted limbs from my yard.
Today I walk to it, press my fingers
on its trunk, the bark rough, warm, and still hard.

The Owls of Allendale

Angels almost, off-white in charcoal rafters,
Planetary above the diesel grit of the barn,
Scent of well-worn tools, voles, hardened
Bags of cement, blink and eavesdrop over
Girlhood stretching her fingers into the lip

Of a coffee can to scrape the twisted ribs
Of leftover screws and the something
Soft reared back in there. Do they suffer
In their forest of joists, heads tilting
Drawn moon faces to read how peppers

And sweet root the shape of a lady
Can be filched, slipped like garnets
In a mouth, when every reach of her
Long thin wrist, her frailing thumb, draws
A fingernail trigger closer to the cache

Half-aware and with fangs? To keep out
Night, the bedroom bulbs silver through
Red hankies her father stuffs into the glass
Dome ceiling fixtures. He turns silhouette
And halo for the girl who asks *who?*

Messengers lock their coin purse beaks,
And, waking, she lifts the glass to her face,
Finds inside a wolf spider splayed, who could
Float past her tongue, crescents winking
From her banded legs, and the eyes in orbit.

Resurrection—A Parable

Once we dug far enough and cracked the earth's skin deep enough
and carved a wound long enough that it couldn't heal, rock bled.
And in this blood were chemicals and when these chemicals touched
air and water, they blistered into a biting compound that turned
    rivers
into an orange slurry suffocating everything that clung to rock and
    lived
off water's movement—insects, fish, crayfish, minnows.

Once there was nothing left to dig, once the earth had nothing left
    to give,
engines stopped and rich people fired poor people who dug deep in
    the dark
each day, and declared bankruptcy and moved to another stretch of
    mountain.
    It's dead they said
    Nothing left of value they declared
    You can have it back they called over their shoulder

Birds that lived off of water—heron, geese, osprey, hawks—left.
    But they were sad doing so. They did not want to leave.
In spring shade spread along bank's cooling water, buds breaking
    into
a scorched landscape hoping something would return. Summer grew
    lonely,
its light and heat did nothing but warm water. Trees grew skinnier
    without
mayflies and stoneflies covering their limbs. In autumn, leaves
    swirled, camouflaged

by bleeding rock instead of creating kaleidoscopic masterpieces in
    eddies.
    How mean and thoughtless those maples said
    How sad cried the rhododendron blooms
    How long asked the river birch.
    How whispered the elm

This went on, season after season. Trees giving what they could to
    water,
water doing what it could to churn death into life, apologizing to the
    banks it smudged,
hoping one day they could fill this emptiness that lingered where life
    should be,
that birds would come back and pierce their skin for minnows in the
    shallows,
that they could clean the dirt off a mink's back as she dips into a
    plunge pool.

Then, decades later, something found its way into this water.
Something that soothed the wound. Something close to holy water.
Soon little shivers of light started darting around rocks and trout
    that were hiding
in tributaries ventured back home and birds returned and air was
    filled with flitting bugs
    and the water that was still stained became a scar they learned to
        love.

Years later a human returned with a fly rod and some questions
and tied on a Parachute Adams, cast into a dark pool under a maple
and laughed as a prayer was answered as a brook trout took the fly.
    Somehow they found their way back
    Somehow they reclaimed this dead water
    Somehow a resurrection

Dunbar Creek: perceptions and place

We live next to, above, and with flowing water. Here, streams shape life as in few places in America. To go anywhere here, streams must be crossed, which we now do without thinking, and streams flood, which we do not forget. Here, if you live in a spot otherwise quiet enough, you can hear a stream, conscious of it or not, ambient to your life. You absorb its timbre; your brain knows its tone. Even our way of speaking about an event that happened near a particular stream is telling. We tend to say the incident happened "on" Ten Mile Creek, or "on" Laurel Run, as if someone walked atop the liquid surface, suggesting an intimacy with streams that is regionally unique. Because streams so clearly carved our topography, intimacy extends, here, to the slopes above a stream—its hollow on the local scale, its basin on a broader one.

You can sense intimacy in the way streams here got named. For some, think "branching tree." The North Fork of the South Branch of the Enlow Fork of Wheeling Creek tells you someone was paying attention when they came here. It tells you those who stayed knew to what their lives were connected. What's left of Native language heired other streams their current names, as did people of more recent historical note. Creeks so named carry to us a hint of the past, like the way a stream carries along that tint of mineral scent you can taste as you approach it in early spring, after a winter sniffing sterile wind.

But intimacy does not mean our streams here were, or are, revered. Flowing water buoyed technological advance, but streams were obliged no deference, more likely to become sewers than remain pristine. Some streams absorbed even more fouling, as if their abuse were a set-upon mission instead of coincidental to progress, insults piled on in excess to subdue an uncivilized place where unthinkable things had occurred. I grew up within the basin of a creek so beset. And when I began to think about such things, I wondered if my native stream had been sentenced to that fate early on, indicted by its own name—Dunbar Creek.

We lived in Fayette County, in Pennsylvania's southwest corner, on a modest knob called Rosy Hill at the western flank of Chestnut Ridge, the Alleghenies' western limit. Gist Run gathered itself from two sources, first, a trickle that descended a farm-pond spillway on the Ainsley farm, downslope to the west where, as kids, we dammed it with mud, then breached our work to thrill at the brown torrent churning downstream, risking a chase by farmer Ted, and second, from a larger branch that sidled around Rosy Hill to the east. Neighbor kids and I crossed that eastern branch in the late 1950s on our daily walk, through sheep pasture and woods to Mt. Braddock School, on a bridge my father built by felling two wild cherries over the flow, digging the lopped and butt ends into the banks, then nailing on boards and a rail. These two "cricks" joined to form Gist Run at Mt. Braddock then flowed north to Dunbar Creek at Dunbar Borough. Some miles farther down, and north, Dunbar Creek enters the Youghiogheny River at Connellsville.

Dunbar Creek was named for Thomas Dunbar, a colonel in British General Edward Braddock's 1755 campaign against the French at Fort Duquesne, built at the confluence of the Allegheny and Monongahela rivers, site of present-day Pittsburgh.

Gist Run is another namesake of these events. Christopher Gist, the first white settler west of the Alleghenies, built a homestead on what would become Gist Run somewhere near where my father built our wild cherry footbridge to school. Knowing the terrain, Gist guided Virginia Governor Dinwiddie's envoy, George Washington, beyond the mountains in 1753 to warn French garrisons to vacate English claims. Washington was rebuffed.

Braddock made his final push northwest over the ridges from Wills Creek, now Cumberland, MD. To speed the advance, he divided his army, leading a "flying force" of 1,200 British regular troops and Virginia militia rapidly off the heights into the Monongahela Valley (the Valley of Death?) and assigned Dunbar to command the slow trudge of artillery, wagons, and more than half Braddock's original strength. But when Dunbar reached the crest of Chestnut Ridge, he met the terrified, bloodied survivors of Braddock's rout by a smaller force of French and their Indian allies, streaming back from the carnage. Mortally wounded, Braddock died during the retreat and was buried in the crude road.

I think about Dunbar and Braddock when I top Chestnut Ridge, most often by car, on a clear fall day, and see Pittsburgh's crisp urban skyline on the northwest horizon. They could not have known, by sight, the precise location of their fateful destination, as I can now. They would have beheld an unmarked ocean of random hills, wherein somewhere lie the Forks of the Ohio River, flowing west to the continental interior.

Dunbar had men and equipment for a counterattack, which might have made the difference in the campaign's outcome. Instead, he burned all the supplies and joined Braddock's decimated remnant in retreat. Braddock's disaster and Dunbar's flight left the English frontier's scattering of settlers exposed to two decades of lethal raids by Indians hoping to hold onto their hunting lands and homes. Resentment over that vulnerability lingered until it diffused in the hum of the Industrial Revolution more than a hundred years later.

Every resource that served industrial awakening could be found in and gleaned from Dunbar Creek's basin. Timber was first to go and the most wholly exhausted. Workable, durable American chestnut climaxed the primal forest, lending its name to Chestnut Ridge from which the creek springs. Chestnut and oak wood framed factories and mills, and hemlock bark streamed into tanneries. The rest of the timber went into charcoal mounds to feed iron furnaces, an acre of woods per furnace per day, and later into coal mines as posts. For decades, any tree, regardless of species, that grew to a size that could prop up a mine shaft was cut and hauled underground. Sandstone boulders, once cloaked by forest, stood out on shorn slopes like grounded arks.

Narrow-gauge railroads probed up the hollows to carry in laborers and haul out timber, stone, clay, iron, and coal. Along the creek's lower reaches, railcars dumped their loads of refuse slag from the furnaces onto the floodplain, sealing the earth under an ossified gray shell that, in places, still caps the soil. When coke replaced charcoal as the fuel of choice in iron and steelmaking, the already fevered extraction of coal erupted. The vaunted Pittsburgh bituminous seam, the world's highest-quality metallurgical coal, was nine feet thick under a third of western Pennsylvania, a thousand feet deep and out of reach. But along a northeast-southwest tangent at the western foot of Chestnut ridge, centered where Dunbar Creek emerges from the mountains, its subterranean pitch thrusts the Pittsburgh seam to the surface, where the mining technology of the day—human muscle and mule—could labor in a honeycomb of shallow but gas-seething, post-propped shafts to drill, blast, pick, and shovel it into mine wagons.

Most of the coal from the Pittsburgh seam went into coke, the remains of coal that had been baked in long straight rows of "beehive" ovens made from fireproof brick. By 1920, forty-thousand coke ovens lit the Fayette County night lurid orange, blotting the noon sun in smoke. Most of those ovens lined the Youghiogheny valley and lower Dunbar basin.

Slate looks something like coal but is not, and young boys learned to know the difference. They picked through the coal as it came out of the shafts and heaped the worthless slate onto spoil piles around the mines. Coal dust in the piles caught fire to smolder and glow dully by night, so that even during my adolescence, snow never laid on the reeking mounds. Nothing I have seen since resembles so precisely those scorched "red dog" mountains as do photographs from the surface of Mars. Decades before my parents forbade me to play near the dumps because "you'll break through and fall in" (to the inferno's core), Fayette County was at the nexus of natural resources and a voracious appetite for them from the Pittsburgh mills. Dunbar Creek's basin was the heart of that nexus. So, despite my naïve musings, and in fairness to Colonel Dunbar, the basin's subjugation had nothing to do with avenging Indian raids. It all would have happened that way even had Dunbar rallied, attacked the French, and emerged victorious at the Forks of the Ohio.

Males in my family had worked at the nexus as coal miners, coke rakers, firebrick kiln tenders and part-time hill farmers, and were glad for it. But by the mid-1960s when boys no longer picked slate at the mine mouth or carried water buckets to the coke oven tenders, my early acceptance into their society came mostly through hunting and fishing, though I did help my grandfather with butchering, haying, and the last of the cattle. My first sorties to fish and hunt with these men struck me as profound. Most were flinty, sometimes grim men whose ingrained concern was whatever work needed or could be done at any moment. Heavy work was supreme creed to my forebears. But when they took me to the woods for deer or grouse or trout, they were like boys, an easy bliss on their weathered faces. I sense now that their release in the woods was my nod to explore, think about, and share what remained of the basin's natural character.

By the time I was old enough to roam the hollows alone, with fly rod or shotgun, a visitor who didn't know what to look for might never notice the vestiges of industrial boom in the basin, especially in the wilder Dunbar headwaters where the ruin had been less complete.

Demand for mine posts withered, so except for chestnut, the woods had grown back, so that you could walk all day and never emerge from the trees. Charcoal mounds were still there if you knew how to see them, covered by sapling and fern, their contours worn. The old rail lines that followed the creeks were blurred by leaf-fall and frost heave, veiled in hemlock overhang, so they seemed placed there as footpaths instead of rights-of-way for steam-belching engines. A high adventure then was to ride those traces bareback on mangy ponies, imagining myself a western explorer. Even the iron furnaces, placed deep in the woods near the last of the charcoal sources, had slumbered to sulking stacks of expertly cut stone, lending oddly square ledges to sun-basking copperheads.

Gist, the run we lived on, is a peripheral, peopled tributary that enters Dunbar Creek well downstream. But the headwaters rise from a remote bowl girded by ledges that soar over jumbled talus. Mountain laurel traces the cliffs above rich woods, where trees of northern and southern pedigree mix. Beech, birch, and maple cling from that colder age when the face of glaciers loomed a hundred miles north. Magnolias, yellow poplar, and sweet buckeye pioneered from the south in the wake of Pleistocene thaw to thrive in sheltered hollows. White, red, or rock oaks, likewise southern, are everywhere, spread by seed-caching jays.

Brook trout were my prized quarry, then as now, and if you have held a wild brook trout across your wet palm in the fall, when it displays its spawning dress, fiery orange belly under slick olive back, speckled across all that in robin egg blue, you know at least one of my reasons for that objective. Yet, I remember being drawn to the contrast between the trees' stalwart permanence and the ephemeral delicacy of wildflowers, so that in spring I often broke down my trout rod to comb the slopes. The bloom was hidden at first, trailing arbutus and hepatica, low and shy on southern exposures. I'd sometimes lay prone on the canted ground and press my nostrils down among dry leaves against an arbutus bloom, sniffing for its clear sweetness. When I'd indulge in such a thing I thought of my grandfathers, laboring in dank darkness or searing heat, with some embarrassment, sensing it was a pleasure they could not have allowed themselves.

Days later gushed the exuberance of bloodroot, trout lily, Dutchman's breeches, and bellwort, then trillium that blanched ravine and streambank white. Enthralled, I marveled at the absence of crowds there to behold it all.

That marvel foretold an encounter. I was fishing with intent, a far hike upstream from the end of the road. The chattering creek muted other sound, so I didn't notice the intent troop approaching from behind me. Startled by a near voice, I turned to see two-dozen people dressed differently than the rare person I encountered back there. Their clothing looked new, even crisp, and seemed purposed, neutral-green or khaki. Some men and women gripped walking staffs, but they all looked fit, wearing newish good boots. Their ages ranged, but all were older than I was. None were missing limbs, a common lacking among older men of my experience. Binoculars swung from necks or a magnifying glass dangled by a tether. Most carried a small book, or some journal stuffed in a pocket.

They were loosely fanned out along the streambank, and they cast their eyes over the ground ahead of their steps, the way my grandfather did when he took me into the woods for morels. Those people were interested in something, to the point of consulting guidebooks and sharing observations, but they carried not a sack among them. Whatever they sought, it bore no immediate utility to be cut, dug, or collected. This, like their clothes, set them apart.

They were friendly and curious about my fishing, so we talked. I learned they were embarked on the annual spring outing of the American Violet Society. They had assembled from across the country to explore the slopes along Dunbar Creek because, as their leader told me, its headwaters held one of the most diverse suites of native violets in North America. Like the trees, various wild violets had either migrated there, or clung on as holdouts, across thousands of years.

Learning such a thing about one's home ground, one's native creek basin, from a stranger from far away is a jar. In the way that my dad's and my uncles' missing work to take me grouse hunting gave me permission to enjoy the woods, the American Violet Society's acclaim for the basin's flora framed it as an exceptional place. Their pilgrimage pushed the slate dump smolder into its historical perspective. Since that day, I have reveled in the Dunbar Creek basin's ecological resilience.

The ecology of any one place is complex beyond easy appraisal. Yet, some of the basin's living elements stand out to me as icons, a word I avoid because of its glib overuse, but it fits the purpose here.

Not everywhere, but at some scattered outcrops, if you climb up from the creek into cool shadows of boulders big as houses, you will be standing at the northern limit of the range of the green salamander, *Aneides aeneus*. This obscure amphibian hunts slugs and beetles in moist sandstone crevices across a range centered on the southern Appalachians, hub of the Earth's greatest radiation of salamander species. Green salamanders' bodies are compressed top-to-bottom, flattened, to fit tight spaces. They shelter within boulders and cliffs from north Alabama, across eastern Tennessee, and along West Virginia's high spine. But they occur nowhere on Earth north of the Dunbar Creek basin in Fayette County, Pennsylvania. Here, at this one point along the 39th Parallel, they stake their extreme reach, where their need for cool, moist rock voids is last met, some individuals living out their lives within 40 feet of the crevice where they hatched. I wonder how they survived the logging boom and the mine-post shearing, when sun must have baked their grottos. But this 3-inch creature's survival here proves the intact roots of natural integrity. Some semblance of best outcome is still possible here.

Wood warblers present the same testimony. Waves of them—more than two-dozen species—enliven the canopy every spring. Some pass on northward to fan out across vast Canadian spruce to breed. After their southward fall journey, all spread widely to winter across the Gulf Coast or in tropical jungle. But here, because they need forest, they are confined to a narrow corridor along the Chestnut and Laurel ridges, whose woods funnel their flight just as an hourglass tapers the passage of sand.

Many, the black-throated blue, magnolia, and blackburnian warblers among them, end their migration here to nest. Small birds, yet so significant by their presence, the warblers are not easily known. This seems a tragedy, but a just one. Foliage obscures them, and they seldom hold still—effort, here, yields great reward. Yet, to the resolute observer, they present such an array of colors, such varied patterns, that, shown pictures, the unfamiliar would assign them to some exotic place—Australia or a Pacific archipelago, to be known only from televised nature documentaries. To see these birds as they are, in early May, I have often climbed atop the same boulders that harbor green salamanders. From there, I could watch the warblers forage through the canopy at eye-level with the light upon them, rather than silhouetted against the sky from below, which renders their plumage featureless black, anonymous.

I am not adept at knowing birds by song. But when I climb the boulders to gape at warblers, I can teach myself to recognize their calls by watching and hearing in the moment, at least for a year, when I must relearn. If I watch a male black-throated blue posturing along a branch, then stop to thrust out his breast in wheezy buzzing song, I will recognize that song later that spring when I'm fishing for trout. I'll know a black-throated blue is somewhere nearby in the hemlocks, even if I never see him, which is as satisfying as the tug of a fish.

Except for wild brook trout, nothing symbolizes for me the basin's wildness, its contrast to towns, like the timber rattlesnake. They're still there on some of the ledges. Somehow, they survived the logging, the fires, blasting their dens with dynamite, and two-hundred years of shooting on sight to wind in and out of the laurel shade as it suits them, almost impossible to see when sun-and-shadow fall across their rough, chevroned hide. They are protected now by legal constraint of the state, which means nothing to some. Still, if they made it this far it seems likely some will remain, unaware that they represent for me both the native rightness of a place, and my own evolving enlightenment.

I once shot a rattlesnake. I cannot explain why except to say that, at that time, where I lived, we never thought of reacting to a rattlesnake in any other way.

We had been riding ponies across the mountain when .22 shots and yells drew our attention. I dismounted and walked toward the shooting among heaped rock piles of an old quarry. A school chum and his father were probing around in the rock slabs, picking off rattlers with head shots where they found them coiled. While I watched, they shot a half-dozen and dragged the limp carcasses out into the sun with long sticks. How can something be so visually striking—velvety black slashed across sulfur yellow—when dragged out of context onto featureless rock, yet be so hard to see when coiled, alive under dappled shade?

Later I returned with two friends and our own .22s. We could find no rattlers in the quarry but happened onto an undisturbed outcrop, capped by laurel and huckleberry, in the woods nearby. When I stepped out of sassafras shade onto a flat shelf of rock, a rattlesnake that had been sunning beneath the shelf uncoiled in a dash for shelter under the slab. Its head was already safe under the rock, so I aimed and shot it mid-body, which showed no effect except that the snake began to rattle, a dry, chitinous buzz that sounds like nothing else. The muffled buzz continued under the rock for a long time, and it claimed my remorse.

I never knowingly harmed another rattlesnake, though I now understand that what I did for a time had the same effect as a rifle. My closest friend and I hunted and caught many rattlers alive. I know this had something to do with a drive to be among, part of, the wildest essence of the Dunbar Creek basin. You had to go to those kinds of places to find rattlesnakes, ledges tucked into rough terrain, blazing hot if you stood in the sun, reached only by long uphill hikes that nobody else attempted.

We displayed our captives in a cage out front of Rippling Waters, a kind of café and grill that was rustic before places tried to be, beverage service "unofficial," built around the walls of a defunct stone-crusher on the banks of Dunbar Creek. Tourists headed for the mountains by the "back way"—somehow before GPS—gawked at the rattlers coiled behind screen before venturing inside, or onto the back porch overlooking the creek, to take a seat among local trout fishermen, snake hunters, and ginseng pickers, and pipeliners up from the flat country of Texas and Oklahoma, fearless in their straddling D9 dozers to strap natural gas transmission lines over the steepest slopes they'd ever worked. Visitors got a delight on weekends when sturdy, aged men from the surrounding hills played fiddle, banjo, and guitar in their understated "old-time" style.

Although I knew most performers, could claim kinship to some, I craved their deeper acceptance. I played no instrument, so what felt like my way into fraternity was to supply rattlesnakes for the cage, which likely evoked amusement more than admiration. Since then, I learned that if you take a timber rattlesnake from its natal range and fail to return it to the same spot within a short time, the snake is doomed. Malnourishment is common in captivity, and a snake released in the wrong place won't find its way back to its winter hibernacula before cold weather. We did release our rattlers but didn't understand the importance of placing them back in the precise spot of capture. Females take eight years to reach sexual maturity. Gestating a born-alive litter is so taxing that they must bask in the sun for hours and weeks to stoke their metabolism, making them vulnerable to predation—and human capture. Those facts suggest that most of the snakes we took in our ignorance were gravid females, and our impact on the local population severe. Today, I return to the rattlesnake ledges infrequently, and only with a camera.

After so many references to brook trout, it may come as a surprise that, ichthyologically speaking, the brook that still inhabited the Dunbar basin when I began to fish there did not include trout, but char of the genus *Salvelinus*. There are deeper differences, but most evident to the human eye is that trout—like the rainbow and brown trout (genus

Salmo)—carry dark spots over a lighter background. Chars exhibit the opposite, showing lighter markings over a dark field. Pale-yellow, worm-like squiggles cover a brook trout's dark- or olive-green back. Char are northern fish of the circumpolar Arctic. The brook trout's nearest kin is the Arctic char, a fish of treeless tundra, fished by Eskimos, its sea-run populations pursued by seals slid from ice-floe lairs. To the south, somewhere this side of the Canadian tree-line, the chars blend into brook trout. They are native to the Dunbar Creek basin because the elevation along the Appalachian chain keeps streams cold enough to support them here near the southern limit of their North American range. The brook trout, then, represents a geographic opposite to the green salamander. Both are reaching to their extremes here, pushing the envelope of toler-ance, the salamander from the near south, and the trout/char from the far north. But nothing about the evolution of char in the Arctic prepared them for Appalachian coal mining.

If you were to look at the color-keyed map, prepared by the Eastern Brook Trout Joint Venture (various fisheries agencies and conservation organizations of the eastern states) to show the status of wild brook trout populations in subdivided watersheds across its native range in the United States, you would see mostly red, indicating "Greatly reduced." The brook trout's American range (excluding where it has been introduced, presenting an invasive threat to native trout, in the Rocky Mountains) covers New England, upland watersheds of the Great Lakes, and most of New York state. Southward, the range funnels across Pennsylvania, broad in the north, tapering to a narrow band along the mountains in the southwest, the same taper the warblers follow in spring and fall. It continues to narrow across West Virginia and into the south-ern Appalachians. Red dominates that whole reach, with vast swaths of murky grey— "Extirpated"—around the margins.

A scatter of green ("Intact") flecks the map across northcentral Pennsylvania, headwater sources of the Allegheny River and the Susquehanna's West Branch, and last best stronghold for the brook trout in northern Appalachia. Dunbar Creek's basin is red, except for titillating smears of yellow, meaning "Reduced," a slightly preferable status to "Greatly reduced." Brook trout are present, but not what could be expected in an undisturbed watershed. In the mid-1960s, when my father and uncles took me upstream on Dunbar Creek to fish for "natives," they told me the same thing the Eastern Brook Trout Joint Venture map attempts to communicate: among the many tributaries that gather into Dunbar, only two hold native brook trout. These are Dunbar Creek's main stem itself, far upstream where my patriarchs called it "Little Dunbar," and Limestone Run, whose name suggests it benefits, from a trout's perspective, from some geological parenting, unusual here.

By volume, the most important tributary in the basin is Glade Run, contributing half of Dunbar Creek's flow. It meets Little Dunbar at a fork that embraces what remains of the Center Iron Furnace, built in the "point" at the two tributaries' confluence. In a geographic sense it represents the "east branch" of Dunbar, descending through the basin's remote heart, mostly within what is now State Game Land No. 51. My father and uncles were not given to overt aesthetics, but they pronounced it a "God damned shame" that such a "beautiful" stream as Glade Run could not be fished. Their undisguised dismay was one of the strongest signals I ever intercepted from my mentoring kin.

Every time I make the effort now to reach Glade Run, I remember their lament. It takes a considerable hike to get there either way you do it, upstream along Dunbar's main stem, or down off the top. Even without trout it is a place that merits, and rewards, the effort. For one thing, wetlands are rare here, and Glade Run is born in one. It flows out of a winding flat, a glade, part swamp and part marsh, where jutting snags and beaver dams convey a wild northern feel. Wood ducks and wood frogs are at home there. Oak-clad knobs rise above the glade on all sides.

Once Glade Run plunges off its plateau, you would never guess where it got its name. It alternately plumes, silvery-white, over the smoothed lips of boulders, and rests in dark-green pools that absorb and exude the solemnity of hemlock shroud. Rounding any bend presents some new version of the elements of Allegheny Mountain trout streams—frothy cascade, smooth green run, stolid boulder, leaning hemlock, each juxtaposed in a different, yet perfect, arrangement. The friction between flowing water and atmosphere drags a cool current of air down off the mountain with it, so that your cheek feels the caress, like the breath of a small child held close. In one stretch the stream has etched its own bed downward through a broad and strikingly horizontal sandstone plane, so that it forms what you can think of only as a "slot canyon," snaking through stone in a constrained channel 15 feet deep and four feet across. During low flows, you can walk the stream inside an enclosed winding passage, a narrow band of canopy-screened sky overhead and fingertips roughing over grainy cool stone as you go. In a high flow you would be churned to meaty slurry. No other place, in my knowledge, is like it.

Yet, despite its idyllic visage, when I began to fish with my father and uncles, there were no trout in Glade. Their "damned shame" was affirmed in the mid-1990s when faculty and graduate students from California University of Pennsylvania's Environmental Studies program surveyed the stream, finding no brook trout, and scant aquatic insects that could support them. What bugs showed up in the Cal U. seines were those that could tolerate acidic conditions.

Brook trout are the most discriminating of salmonids. They require cold water, the kind that wells up from mountain innards. Glade Run has that, but it must be clean— "clean" being a term that takes in a lot. The chemical properties must be right, there can be no overloads of sediment or nutrient, and there's a fragile balance of acid and base that can't be tipped.

That balance in the Dunbar basin, in fact in most streams across western Pennsylvania, tips easily toward acid. Our region's common geology is stingy in limestone, which, when it's present, blesses streams ushering from it with a property called alkalinity, the "buffered" ability to resist acidification from an external source, like acid rain or a coal mine discharge.

When I was born, in 1952, the initial coal boom in the Dunbar basin was already over. But around that time, bigger and better equipment made surface- or strip-mining feasible to extract lesser (than the Pittsburgh seam) seams whose sedimentary position and the pitch of their uplift made them accessible on the mountaintops without sending men into shafts. Those coal seams cropped out on three sides—north, south, and west—of one of the knobs above Glade Run's wetland birthplace.

The long-abandoned 1950s' strip-mine scars are still up there, across whole slopes, right down to the alder and cattail margins of swamp. You'd recognize the spot anywhere in Appalachia, yellow clay, scraggly alien pine trees stuck in the ground in pale attempts at reclamation, and crude, stony terraces to channel runoff. Sulfuric acid, the predictable brew that forms all across our coal regions when latent underground sulfur contacts the air, coincidental to coal's extraction, seeps or gushes out of the ground in dozens of places. When that acid first hit Glade Run, which lacked buffering limestone, it tipped the balance beyond the brook trout's tolerance. My fishing guides knew that, and when we hiked upstream with our trout rods and reached the forks at Center Furnace, they paused, gazed briefly up Glade Run, clucked their tongues, then turned right to lead me up untainted Little Dunbar.

There was no way, in their time, that my father and uncles could have imagined that anything could be done to remedy Glade Run's malady. Their only available reaction was to lament what might have been. Even now, that default still infects attitudes, so that most people who are aware of the devastation of acid mine drainage assume stream restoration is too great a challenge. But fishing can endear you to a stream for life, and Dunbar Creek was "fishable" below the Glade Run confluence because Little Dunbar diluted the acid enough to allow the state Fish Commission to stock trout there every spring. The principal worth of those hatchery fish was that they survived long enough to hook anglers on the place, some to imagine better possibilities.

I know people who came to care for Dunbar Creek in that way. In 1995, some of them founded the Chestnut Ridge Chapter of Trout Unlimited, affiliate to the national organization committed to conserving and restoring coldwater fisheries.

Chestnut Ridge TU members all shared the view of my ancestors, that Glade Run was too alluring a mountain stream, too otherwise perfect, to be without trout. But they refused to accept that absence as something they could not change. They learned how to sample stream water with protocoled credibility, then hiked throughout the drainage gathering samples. They raised money, gave their time, won grants. They sought technical help from the Western Pennsylvania Conservancy's (WPC) watershed office and waded into the complexity of getting regulatory permits to begin work.

In 1998 they began experimental "dosing" of Glade Run's main stem and two tributaries, Big Piney Run and Little Piney Run, with high-calcium limestone "sand," which is not truly sand, but the finest particles of limestone left on the sizing screens at stone quarries after the stone is crushed for construction uses. The sand is so fine that it mostly dissolves in the water, unleashing the acid-balancing properties the stream's bedrock origins lack.

The dosing improved Glade's pH and its alkalinity. Encouraged, the group placed hatchery brook trout in a cage in the stream. The trout lived, boosting the group's resolve, and justifying more funds.

In 2003 they completed construction of a $300,000 anoxic limestone drain treatment system that captures and neutralizes much of the mine water that discharges into Glade Run. Soon after, teaming with California University of Pennsylvania fisheries biologists, they collected wild brook trout by electro-shocking Little Dunbar Creek, where a population remained, carried the small fish over the divide in watertight backpacks, and released them into Glade Run. Within two years Cal. U. biologists documented natural reproduction and two year-classes of brook trout fingerlings. Brook trout had returned to a secluded creek where they had thrived for 10,000 years, 3,000 miles south of their evolutionary roots, rendered once and briefly inhospitable by the single-minded exposure of coal beds, moved on to another slope above some other stream.

Even after they built the treatment system, the group combed the mined-over slopes looking for more untreated discharges. They found many, so continued the limestone dosing in the Glade Run headwaters for nearly two decades. Their progress attracted more attention from the Western Pennsylvania Conservancy, whose more robust funding network enabled the WPC to build a larger treatment system on the old mine footprint, capturing "hot" discharges that bypassed the first facility. The water's chemical balance improved even more, though some leaching pollution remains to be captured.

In a regulatory initiative unimaginable to the men who took me trout fishing as a boy, the Pennsylvania Department of Environmental Protection proposed in 2018 that the Dunbar Creek basin, including Glade Run and its tributaries, 50 total stream-miles, be designated "Exceptional Value." An Exceptional Value classification places so-designated streams under the state's most vigilant shield of environmental protections. The proposal must run a tortuous bureaucratic and political gauntlet, outcome unknown, but the Exceptional Value proposal itself proves immense achievement.

From the viewpoint of an accomplished trout angler, a person perhaps who can fish where they want in the world—Montana, Argentina, Alaska—Dunbar Creek's main stem is still an under-achieving trout fishery. But it's improving, which says much around here.

More people value the stream now, take pride in its nearness. I remember my own father pulling his Chevy into one of the shallow fords across Dunbar Creek, clear water up to the hubcaps, because it was acceptable then and natural to do. We'd all then pitch into the novel fun of washing our car in the creek, next to big-fendered Dodges and Plymouths whose owners were doing the same thing, our collective sheen of suds, solvents, and wax gliding toward the next downstream riffle. People don't do that anymore, maybe for lots of reasons, but among those is a consensus that to treat a stream in that way is coarse.

Consensus about public spaces is never universal, and as proposed earlier, contact with a stream does not necessarily engender reverence. Some people still ride their ATVs along and through the streams, even on the state game lands where the rules forbid motorized play, strewing beer cans and eroding the banks, burying trout lily in an unctuous gray ooze. Such boorishness is fringe, though, as shown by Trout Unlimited's cleanups along Dunbar Creek on the Saturday before the opening of trout season every April. The group's commitment extends beyond the water's chemical health to include each visiting angler's aesthetic experience.

Through all the years I've fished Dunbar Creek, a dirt road has followed it upstream to a dead-end well below the Glade Run confluence. It's known as Betty Knox Road, named for a spectral heroine of local lore. Betty Knox still walks that road some nights, legend says, calling for her lost lover, a wounded deserter from the Civil War. The road is access for anglers, but it's also the kind of remote dumping-ground some people seek out. Even that pox has improved. The cleanups there once took an entire day and filled three Penndot tri axles (because the cleanup extends downstream to and along SR 1055, the Dunbar-Ohiopyle Road, Penndot agrees to haul collected debris to a landfill) with tires, bottles, cans, and castoff commodes. Now it takes a pickup truck and two hours to make the creek's accessible sections presentable.

For me, the people who worked toward the restoration of Glade Run, and Dunbar Creek downstream, represent a climax to a continuum. It begins with my father, uncles, and some of their friends taking me trout fishing on the still-healthy streams of the Dunbar basin, noting in their understated sadness the spoiling of the most attractive creek of all. Their dismay is illuminated and buoyed by my recall of the American Violet Society field trip I met long ago while fishing. They knew about and sought something that was still there in the basin; not just a wildflower but the natural resilience of a place left to its own, even for a short time, in this temperate part of the world. But that resilience did not extend to streams that lacked the blessing of a limestone birth to temper acidification. Streams needed help to rebound, help that continues. The brook trout's absence from Glade Run, throughout the bulk of my time to live, and fish, diminished the lives of all of us who went there, even the lives of those who did not, because it was an absence from water, and within water flows our link to all ground above, our life's signature carried below.

Postscript

A recent conversation in which I took part hints that for people in some places, perhaps even here, in ways powerful within their lives, contact with, indeed, any knowledge of, flowing water is fading. I share a summary here:

I was helping my aged mother write checks to pay her bills. She had lost the pre-addressed return envelope for one bill and was anxious about what to do. A phone number on the statement invited a call with questions.

"I'll just call this number, tell them you lost the envelope and ask for the address," I assured her.

A courteous young woman answered my call. When I explained our dilemma, she provided the accounts-payable address in Carol Stream, Illinois.

She spoke rapidly, and the town's name was unusual and unfamiliar, so I sought confirmation.

"Is that Carol, like a woman's name?" I asked.

"Yes, Carol, just like a woman's name."

"And is that second word stream, like a small river?" I pressed.

There was silence on the line, then, tentatively, "No," and she spelled it for me. "It's S-T-R-E-A-M, stream, like when you stream a video."

Then I fell silent.

When I'd recovered enough to thank the young woman for her help, I hung up and related the exchange to my mother, who is 93. She is understandably challenged by some abstractions now, but she grasped the significance of the phone receptionist's focus. My mother has never fished in her life, but she knew we kids dammed the outflow from Ainsley's pond because she had fielded Ted's complaints when the breached impoundments chewed at his pasture. She was there when her husband built a bridge across a fork of Gist Run, from wild cherry trees that grew on its banks, to get us kids from "the hill" to school. She has washed a lot of wet, muddy clothes and she knew I could not sleep on the nights before the men took me trout fishing.

She will likely be gone soon, and with her that small piece she held of our collective knowledge of streams as flowing water. The Dunbar Creek basin conferred to her that part of her life. She absorbed it unsought, from a current never ceased.

Somewhere West of Ebensburg

Western Pennsylvania is chain-smoking,
burning its coal, turning black rock to white smoke.
Somewhere west of Ebensburg on Route 22,
there's a "Trump digs coal" sign
left over from the pre-election days of 2016.
Coal-powered plants are puffing white smoke
that spreads out like low clouds
over gently rolling hills.

No pretense or Hollywood glitz out here
where, in the distance, green hills meet the sky,
but there are farms and rusting tractors and trucks,
remnants of earlier times, here and there,
beside the highway.

On 22, people are driving between towns,
to and from work, or to Walmart,
the biggest building and parking lot seen from the road.
Restaurant, hotel, gas station, and fruit market signs
left over from the '50s, '60s, '70s,
faded and weathered,
still stand in front of businesses
that closed years ago.

This rough-around-the-edges region,
from which coal miners and lumbermen
in the 1800s and early 1900s
brought forth tons of coal and lumber—
industries that continue today,

along with manufacturing, tech, and defense—
still works hard to be economically relevant.

Luke Combs' "Blue Collar Boys"
blares from an open window
of a white Ford F-150 parked at a Sheetz,
the big, red convenience store,
where people buy gas, beverages,
made-to-order food, lottery tickets, etc.,
at all times of day and night.
Sheetz stores are big, bright-red
commercial beehives
in these small, rural towns.
Men and women, young and old,
some wearing gold and black
Steelers jerseys or Pirates caps,
pump gas and order sandwiches.
Customers are busy paying for orders,
and picking up hot or cold beverages and food
before hurrying back to their cars,
then back to the road.

Since the 2020 Presidential election,
and the much-viewed blue and red U.S. political map,
the nation, the world, knows this area as red.
Red as the Sheetz stores,
Red as the MAGA hats.
Red as the state motto ribbon
on Pennsylvania's blue state flag:
"Virtue, Liberty and Independence."
Red, Red, RED.

Smoke & Diesel: A Dirge

Weirton Junction, WV 1967

Gathered gargantuan locomotives,
their fuel tanks dark fuselages,
their headlamps yellow fierce piercings
of fog, groan on side-by-side
sidings. Blue fume hovers and broods.
Steam seeps from the mill
like a wail of cats.
Rumbles reverberate between
green-black hills. Nothing
ever rests: all day and all night
the air itself
is pounded thin, then shaken.

This is the price paid,
the tribute required.

River, creek, silence,
hacked-away hillsides
in the great making and taking—

the endless requiems.

Upon Seeing the Signs Along National Road in Wheeling, West Virginia

The morning the teachers walked off the job,
gray rain came down. Mist from the Ohio
pulsed through streets and empty lots, like the throb

of a thumb with a splinter half below
the skin. I could not read the signs as I
drove down the street's center line past the row

of umbrellas, doing my best to try
to avoid hitting the potholes of late
February, to prevent a splash high

enough to flood the curb and saturate
the huddled forms ranged along that sidewalk.
The women James Wright described walking straight

into the river, a baptismal shock
each night, a ritual drowning and rebirth:
those women are not these women. Wright's flock

of bedraggled whores rises to the earth
from a river that is not this river.
No woman can enter and come to berth

twice in the same river. But the river,
flooding its banks, fertilizing the soil,
leaving a trace, even just a sliver

of the drowned ones, the luckless, whose toil
in the water came to no happy end,
the river flows with its grief and turmoil,

cresting, spilling over, intent to spend
itself upon the land, where green shoots,
like the signs on National Road, transcend

the trauma of their birth and, unfurling, ascend.

Caroline Wermuth

Pennsylvania from a Plane

Framed by a green
and brown
patchwork quilt
of farms and fields,
the school buses,
dormant for the summer,
sit like pencils in a box.

In Nomine Patris

My Catholic primary school built a new church and converted the old one into classrooms. The new one isn't connected to the school building. It sits on the back lot behind the gym surrounded by smooth asphalt and strategically placed greenery. Walking across the lot, weaving in and out of cars, my skin feels hot. It's the religion. It's the people inside the religion, the clusters of grieving congregation members floating through the lot with me.

Our group merges with others through the two heavy wooden doors. Mica and Jolene are cut off from the rest of us at the front, then more people file in and cut me off from Ray and Tyler. I keep an eye on Tyler's greasy man bun as the mob shuffles through an impressive lobby with large potted plants, that may or may not be real, and moves toward another set of double doors into the church.

The man in front of me stops. I run into him, smack my nose right against his shoulder. He apologies, nods his head a lot, then dips two fingers in the marble holy water well carved into the wall, blesses himself, and moves on. I don't dip my fingers. I walk up to the table with weekly newsletters and folded funeral pamphlets by the center aisle where my friends wait. The room's vaulted ceilings resemble gothic churches from the 16th century. They contrast the Grecian columns that cut like long teeth through the room and create three distinct sections of pews.

It all seems wrong. Too big. Too open.

People in black armed with tissues and rosaries dangling from their fists pepper the pews. Towards the front, teachers and nuns stand in their own circles.

"Where should we sit?" Jolene glances this way and that. The stray strands that fall out of her hair clip sway; a single hair gets caught on her plastic nose ring.

"I don't see anyone we know," Ray says. "Let's go over there." He points to the right side of the church, to the collection of empty back pews where only latecomers and people with screaming babies sit.

We sit too close to each other at the aisle end of a pew three from the back. The clay relief of Jesus emerging from a stone tomb watches us from the wall between two skinny stained-glass windows. Stragglers looking for their parties and nuclear families linger on us, as one would seeing a toddler sitting at a bar.

We didn't know that eighth grade graduation would be the last time walking out of the place, but fifteen years passed and suddenly we're back. I see some distinct faces in the clusters, but they feel more like storybook characters, like far away people who have never significantly interacted with my life.

Jolene doesn't feel the same. She taps each of us several times to point out our old teachers or classmates, to reminisce about student council elections, classroom shenanigans, and the underage drinking scandal that we may or may not have participated in. Her memories are clear, detailed, even fond. Mine gather like sand dunes shifting in a haboob.

"I hate this thing," Jolene whispers, playing with the clear plastic post in her left nostril.

"I told you not to wear it," Mica says.

"I couldn't wear my hoop to church." Jolene's lips pucker. "And if I don't wear anything then the hole might close."

"It wouldn't close in an hour," Mica says.

"How would you know?"

Ray and Tyler have their phones out on the other side of Jolene. Anything they say is covered by Jolene and Mica's third spat of the morning. I turn away from them, lock eyes for a moment with a pregnant woman passing by, nod politely, watch her waddle up the aisle and genuflect—to the best of her swollen ability—before shimmying into a pew.

Behind the altar hangs the larger-than-life crucified Jesus recycled from the old church, where it took up most of the back wall. Here it's dwarfed by intricate tile work and Latin phrases scrawled beneath the crown molding. I used to be afraid of the statue; I thought it would fall on me when I sang in the choir. Every few lines, I'd look up to make sure it was still bolted to the wall, then I'd wonder why someone would carve that stupid look on his face. It isn't a dying man's expression. It's exhaustion, maybe, but nothing more than that. The eyes slop to the side and the skin sags around his jaw, like the artist carved it out of wax then left it out in the sun too long.

A grand piano strikes up the beginning lines of "Amazing Grace." It's probably the only song I still know by heart. The music bounces off the marble and echoes into the far corners. Only a few spots in the nave are empty, and most of the side pews are full-up. The crowd's made of different nationalities and generations. The looks on their faces are all the same, though. It's a little like Jesus' above the altar.

It's a long procession in. First the bishop; then the practicing priest; then a brood of altar boys carrying Bibles and golden statues on sticks and pushing along the light brown coffin; then several family members trailing behind. I shouldn't be surprised to see family with Father Wert's remains, but it doesn't always make sense when you think about priests having anyone but God to keep them company. Then again, none of this makes any sense to me. Not this church. Not these superstitious rituals. Not me sitting here.

I stopped believing in God the way I stopped believing in Santa Claus: one minute He was real, and the next He wasn't. It was in second grade during one of Father Wert's homilies. At least, I think that's when it happened. Father Wert was talking about Cain and Abel, relating it to our daily lives, to the bad things happening in the world, to the murder of a teenager a couple days before, and God suddenly didn't exist. I remember looking down at the missal in my hands, paging through the songs of praise, and thinking that all of it was a lie. I remember looking around at my class and the kids older than me and the first graders in front of me and wanting to say something, but having no idea how to form the words. I feel the same way now, listening to the Bishop start his sermon, watching the people sit and stand and turn to page 347 to sing along with the choir. I don't stand. I get some sideways glances from a group of women in the pews across the aisle. I think about telling them God is like Santa Claus.

Jolene smacks my arm and jabs her head toward me, the way mother ducks do to threaten their ducklings.

Even when I stand, her gaze pierces me.

Mica chuckles and bumps my shoulder. "Mom's mad," he says.

"She doesn't get to be mad when she looks like she's picking her nose."

We both glance sideways at Jolene, her thumb nestled in her nose fixing the plastic stake, her free hand still holding Mica's. We giggle, and for a moment this place feels natural. The ground, the walls, the way Tyler's foot fiddles with the folded up kneeling bench—it's familiar, comfortable even. It takes me back to sixth grade and sneaking cookies into Father's classes on Monday mornings.

Jolene smacks Mica's shoulder and snaps him back to attention. He sucks his lips into his mouth and bites back the laughter.

"You guys are assholes," she whispers.

"No cussing in church," Mica says with the cadence of an actual sixth grader.

Even with several pews between our group and the vertically-nearest grievers, a woman looks back at us, the wrath of a PTO council member in her eye. Like good Catholic boys and girls, we bow our heads in apology and turn our attention to the bishop.

A funeral is just Mass with some extra words and more readings about death. The bishop's speeches are pretty. He knew Father Wert, and says nice things about him and his dedication to the Church and the school. "The righteous perish," he reads from Isaiah or Joshua, though I can't quite hear him over the nose-blowing, "and no one takes it to heart; the devout are taken away," he pauses to stare provocatively at the congregation, "and no one understands that the righteous are taken away to be spared from evil. Those who walk uprightly enter into peace; they find rest as they lie in death."

We get to Communion after only three songs, four readings, and two of Tyler's "bathroom" breaks. The teachers and nuns present the gifts as a group. My first grade teacher carries the wine. I can't remember her name, but I remember the time my friend told her that the Bible isn't real because no one has a last name.

They set the gifts on the altar in front of the bishop and the school's current priest. The way the priest waves his hand over them for a blessing is strict, like a blade cutting the air. He passes out wine and wafers to four others who position themselves around the church to catch people in need of Jesus. My stomach growls; it's an automatic response after so many years of morning Mass without breakfast.

The choir starts up a high-frequency rendition of a tired communion song. Patrons pass me, sparing glances or awkward smiles. Some nod in recognition, and I nod back whether I know them or not. I look down the row for anyone who may want to get up. Ray leans back and plays on the phone nestled between his knees. Tyler looks at me; the sides of his mouth pull up until his red eyes are barely open, and he giggles. Jolene perches on the edge of her seat and watches the patrons shuffle from their pews into black lines. She sits like this until the people before us file out, then she leans back and draws on the back of Mica's hand with her nail. Mica guesses she's drawing a penis several times before she gives up and folds her arms. I pull the missal tucked into the wooden basket on the back of the pew in front of me and page through the songs. Most of them are the same I sang in choir. For some, I can remember the tunes and hum along in my head.

There's still a lot of crying, a lot of red eyes and sad looks. One man changes course on his way back from communion and detours past Father Wert's coffin. He places his hand on the light wooden lid as he passes. Like lemmings, those behind him follow the new path rounding Wert's coffin and touch the side or top as the first man did. Only a few of us are sitting: A boy a few pews up who subconsciously clutches the shirt around his upper arm. An elderly woman in a wheelchair halfway up the next row. A surprising amount of people from the Egyptian family who owns the 24-hour diner by the mall, including Leo from our graduating class.

Communion ends as the last recipients file into the pews and take a knee to thank God and ask for favors. A woman behind me whispers her prayers out loud, asks God to protect her grandchildren. From what, she doesn't say.

I think about telling her that God is too busy for those things. That if God really exists, He doesn't have time to make sure Tommy and Suzy have a fun vacation to the beach or to make sure your dog recovers from pneumonia. He has real problems, like the war in Iraq or the hundreds of priests in His Church convicted of molestation or world hunger.

I weigh the probability of these things while the priest and bishop suck down the rest of the wine and put the untouched bread in the golden tabernacle. The bishop readjusts his white silk hat, and the red fringes on the end of its lappets tickle his ear. He gestures for the congregation to stand for another sing-song phrase and then sit to listen to Wert's sister read a long piece of the Bible. She relates it to Father Wert's love for the Church, his love for God, his dedication to Christian education.

Ray and I lean back to exchange a brief look behind everyone else's heads.

When you get out of your small town and gain a bit of wisdom, you realize the parts that were wrong and right about your upbringing. You think back on your parents, their punishments and rewards, the times you did well and the times you didn't, the things you were led to believe and the people who believed them. Father Wert did educate us during Mass and his religion classes. He taught us Genesis to the Disciples, the crucifixion, the plagues, the righteousness, and then he taught us about Hell, about the people who go there and the demons who play there and the sins that would get us sent there. Maybe that's why my clearest memory of Wert is on the day I stopped believing, and after that he became like a tumbleweed rolling between the shifting dunes.

Wert's sister closes her notes, bows to the altar, and goes back to the front pew. She wobbles on her heels stepping off the platform. While the Bishop calls on the Lord to take Wert's soul through the pearly gates, I contemplate the social constructs of gender norms and expectations of funeral attire. Some people aren't in black. I've seen it as a growing trend: wearing bright colors to funerals. I'm not sure it means anything. Maybe they don't own black. Maybe they're trying to break expectations. Maybe the man three pews up just really enjoys that salmon polo.

Everyone stands. The organ strikes up. They sing a song I've never heard. Jolene doesn't notice me this time, and I'm grateful because the world's different when you're sitting in a crowd of people standing. It all seems a bit clearer. I imagine this is how it feels to be a child, though I don't remember those feelings myself. I don't remember the first funeral I went to, but I know I didn't cry because my mom told me, and I know it was after I stopped believing in God. Maybe that's why I didn't cry, or maybe that's why I should have. Is it better or worse to think you'll see someone again? I wonder where, if there is an afterlife—Heaven and Hell—Father Wert ended up.

It's nice to think all priests go to heaven, but we know what some priests do to kids and we hope no one like that gets eternal paradise.

Then again, if a priest can be damned, what hope is there for the rest of us?

Ray leans over Tyler's lap. "We don't have to go to the cemetery, do we?"

"The program says they're doing a private burial for the family," Mica says.

"Good," Tyler says, "then let's go get food after this."

"Let's go get a *drink* after this." Ray scratches the two-day old stubble on his chin.

When I told my parents I stopped believing in God, my confession came out more as an accusation: "Why'd you let me believe something so stupid?" That's why they sent me to Father Wert after Mass on Sundays for the entire summer. They would go to lunch at a restaurant across the street and leave me in the rectory with him and my Bible and this endless swelling of piano music that crackled on his record player. To this day I can't listen to Bach or Beethoven without craving a cigarette.

His skin smelled like the musk incense they burn in churches and candle wax on parchment, the way university libraries and leather notebooks in the sun smell. His hands sort of felt like that, too: old and papery. The skin sagged off his knuckles and the gold ring on his right pinky twisted each time he turned a page. We started with a detailed explanation of the commandments, which he insisted on reading only in Hebrew or Latin, and continued through the Old Testament book by book, parable by parable, until the pages' corners wore thin under his licked thumb.

The bishop leads the processional down the aisle and out of the church as the song dwindles to its final chords. The pews empty from the front to the back, one long line after another. The music stops before the nave is clear.

A middle-aged man with thick blonde hair at the back of the church says, "Father Wert's family invites all of you to join them in the cafeteria for sandwiches and coffee, which was generously donated by the school in honor of Father Wert's many years of service."

Father Wert didn't answer my questions about why he couldn't prove God's existence or why people in the Bible didn't have last names. He only told me that God never gives us more than we can handle and that as long as we follow God's laws, we will all live forever. After three months, I told my mom and dad that I believed in God again so I wouldn't have to stay after Mass anymore.

A man with crutches gets stuck trying to get out of his pew in front of us. Mica shoves me into the sudden gap in the crowd and tows Jolene, Tyler, and Ray with him. It's a crawl across the back of the church and a traffic jam at the double doors where people pause to bless themselves again.

Ray sticks all four fingertips into the holy water as he passes and makes the sign of the cross. "Spectacles, testicles, wallet, and watch."

Tyler's smile stretches up his face. "Ha!" He giggles to himself. "Spectacles, testicles . . ."

"You are such children," Jolene groans. She pulls Mica by his hand through the inconveniently placed pockets of people and out into the parking lot. "So, food?"

"Food," Tyler sighs. "Yes, food, please."

"Nothing too expensive," I say.

"There's that pub like five minutes that way." Jolene points beyond the highway that sweeps behind the church toward the outer limits of town.

"I don't care as long as there's beer and cheese fries," Ray says.

"Cheese fries . . ." Tyler echoes.

One Morning (Crawford Township)

One morning, someone pounded the door so hard it bent
inward a little at the upper corner opposite the hinges—

Edward, Jr., panting, beet-faced, running sweat, hay clippings
plastered to jiggly chest & arms *shear bar came loose   knives flew*

by my head   heckuva mess out there so of course I let him
call his mother to get *Billy to come get me* & got him a beer,

but he stomped back out to the tractor the uncut alfalfa
half-hid & lickety-split Billy lolled a huge Chrysler up the field

& off they went. For two days, no engines, though the cicadas
did their best. Nothing can do justice to the blackbirds & fireflies.

Arneman Road

The saddest of the four Franks I've known
said we lived in the roadkill capital of the world

& was kind to me when I was a stranger.
Bedeviled by woodchucks, I'd pour ammonia

down a burrow, shovel the dirt back in
& stomp the plugged hole concrete-hard

till the abject helplessness in which I seethed
drove me to my knees to weep. Nothing

digs like a gopher. Oh, schizophrenic Frank,
wandering around Utica. Here we briefly lived.

That Summer

death hung in the air
a sickly-sweet smell

so distinct
and uncommon to modern lives

the brief assault of skunk or possum
assailing nostrils at sixty miles per hour

the bloated doe, eyeless, opened, at the side of the road
attended by undertakers in their feathered, dark robes

but that summer death kept coming to us
six raccoons, a groundhog, the spotted fawn

our dogs reverting to a bloody pack
carrion covering the lawn

we came to know maggots and beetles
the way a body collapses upon itself

how fur and bone remain
long after flesh is gone

the dogs lounged in the garden
crunching wild jaws and thighs

we picked cups of teeth instead of flowers.

Farming Ways and City Kids

JC Dunlap Farm, Cadiz, Ohio 1969

We join Grandpap on the side porch, rocking in
unison. I remark that I forgot to put the hose away,
when calmly Pap rises from his chair and says "Never
you mind about that—your Gram wants you," and
sends us inside.

Watching through the door, we see him take out a huge
gray pistol and shoot that hose into two parts near one
end. Gram clucks into her apron, hovering around us in
the kitchen.

Grandpap brings the hay tractor up to the driveway, rolls
and rolls and rolls that hose—once, twice, seven times,
then throws it onto the wagon's silver planks. He salutes
Gram as she prays that there isn't a nest nearby, mutters
that Mom will never let us come back to the farm.

My cousin says that snakes travel in pairs, making my sister
cringe. Gram says lightning kills more people than snakes,
and they only get together to mate. Grinning, my little brother
grabs his cigar "nature box" and slams out the screen door. His
6'6" boy body lopes down the lane after the tractor, anticipating
a snake head for his collection.

I Don't Know How to BE Appalachian

but I know how a transmission hunkers down to climb curved, oil-covered gravel roads carved into mountain edges, how ears pop with elevation and chewing gum is the solution. I know the scent & sound of thousands of pines, how to respect the rhythms of seasons & soil, to prepare for change. How primal need traces wandering roots. The sound of a vowel. **APPLE A SHUN.**

I don't know how to **be** Appalachian. All those assumptions about normalcy: Clampetts & McCoys, moonshine & edentulousness, bare feet & church snakes. Drawls, & "yinz" & "pridnears." Food stamps & illiteracy.

I don't know how to **be** Appalachian, only the way **I say** Appalachian when I mean **home**, pinprick on a map. One road settlement, County Road 14, where generations of my people were born & died in the same bed in the same house, starting when hope & chutzpah spurred them to cross mountains, forge a river.

How my grandmother lived in a house without plumbing, the house where she was born, my father & uncles were born, her mother was born, & on back. How their log living connected to the first post office, general store, hostelry, smithy. A ten-cent barn stabled a horse all day with a bucket of oats. Before dog-trots. First folks on Farmington Road, home passed down, each generation adding or subtracting: from logs covered by clapboard to asbestos shingles, then vinyl siding. A garage. Out buildings. Porches & arbors that were, & now aren't. Root cellars, gardens, fruit & nut trees, wood & coal stoves, fuel oil heat. Hunting hounds tied outside, washboard & wringer. Wells & privies. Slop buckets, compost buckets, family water buckets with dippers, gut buckets, wash buckets.

We are self-reliance, hard labor, bucolic & meditative chores. Star bright stillness of night. Snow on quilts in morning, frost whiskers on ceilings & windows, wool clothes, iron skillets. We put things by, can meat, fruit, & vegetable. Pickle, salt, smoke, & dehydrate. Drain cottage cheese through muslin. Make catsup in enamelware, apple butter in copper. Keep bees, harvest honey. Forage for medicine. Grow kitchen gardens. Know what flowers or mushrooms to eat. How to sort, save, make do. What to burn or repair. How to darn & mend, quilt & weave, sew a screen. Dowse.

I hear the dead remind me of what is old & true. How they will be lost to the next generation.

When I reach for family, I only touch air.

In my Appalachia, the still summer night is holy & profound. There are bullfrogs & tree toads & crickets all around. Smell of green, iron, & sulfur. You hear one truck coming from miles away. Community is the basis of survival, elders expect respect; you hello a house before you visit; all women over twenty are "miz."

I know about shared blood moving inside me like birdsong leaking through windows. I know how to grieve in increments: time we left the mountains, time we visited, time when someone died. I know about home birth, how to be the first of the very first generation born in hospital. 1957—my place in time. MY Appalachia. MY mosaic of rituals: tiny shards of lives where their stars are my galaxies. MY bonds chained with a historic past.

I don't know how to **be** Appalachian, but I know about family trees. Ship manifests. I know about my Patriots who donated forts or crossed the Delaware, wintered at Valley Forge. Hessian mercenaries. Huguenots, Quakers, Methodists, & Lutherans. Indian fighters. Wealthy, landless, skilled, unskilled. Indentured servants. Women who cared for the sick & wounded, cooked, mended, buried the dead, served in combat. Women who stayed alone with children, fought off starvation, weather, wolves & wilderness. Who farmed crops, worked homesteads until their husbands returned. Those who were captured & returned by Indians. I am the commingled genes of those farmers, artisans, leaders, & laborers. My people, paid in mountainous land grants after the war. They are my Apple a sha.

I know we've become so many doors that only open from the inside, pockets of a country who came from the world over, people with little more than a wagon load of dreams & sturdy bodies. An axe, a gun, bullets, garden seeds, salt, flour, dry beans, a knife, whetstone, an iron skillet. People with pluck, drive & dignity. Long gone are those blue-black nights & pure dirt floors; we the people of checkered terraced farmland.

Today we've allowed ourselves to be less community & completely hypnotized by consumerism & technology. We've stopped fact checking, rarely read or question, especially "authority." We've become under-educated, immoral, selfish. We ignore the poor & medically vulnerable. Hate & manipulation have fueled our existence. We have contrived what democracy means. These people are my Apple a sha.

Where goes the pursuit of happiness? It certainly isn't my grandfather's thousands of acres of Herford farming in Cadiz, his 1700's cabins. It isn't the house on his property with secret stairways behind walls leading from underground to attic. It isn't my grandmother's family place in Martins Ferry, where generations were fed directly from its soil, where the windows have wavy glass, & it still belongs to family. I know that Outsiders vs Insiders is an equation I do understand, ("You didn't grow up around here, did you?"). I know that my story & American history are not told with the same words. MY Appalachia. MY Ohio. My anthem. I don't know how to **be** Appalachian, but I know the way.

Listen, America

while I got air enough to speak
what you don't want to hear.
The X-rays of my lungs look like the inside
of a mountain we done mined. Scars built up
around the coal and rock dust I sucked in.
I'll need more than breath to get it out again.
Oh, lordy.
There's no one looks forward to dying.
Listen, America,
just because there ain't no more living
to be made in coal, don't mean the coal
should be taking the life out of me.

Drawn from interviews in "Living With Black Lung—Coal Miners Caught in a Surging
Epidemic." www.ohiovalleyresource.org. Accessed 2 September 2018

You Could Draw a Circle Around Where I'm From

"That's where miners are getting sick
That's where miners are dying.
And anybody who tells you, 'We need more information.'
They're lying."

Found poem spoken by UMW President Cecil Roberts at the West Virginia Black Lung
Association Conference, June 2019.

A Coal Miner's Wife Reads News of the Coronavirus

from a line in Muriel Rukeyser's 1938, The Book of the Dead,
in the spirit of the "golden shovel"

He told me, "A lot of things can get you in the mines.
They want us worrying about another fellow's
sneeze? We're used to coughing up a lung—hell, we're packed
so tight into the mantrip who can even tell whose lung it is.
I'd rather work than not." So, what am I supposed to say to that?
Tell him, the paper says, *in fact last week…coal became*
the most expensive fossil fuel? A fact some wives
have known for years, but we weren't talking dollars.
Coal is so essential it's unbelievable, said the governor
who owns not just the mine but the whole damn state above it.
Unbelievable is right. I'm not one to tell my man or anybody else
to leave a job that's steady, but it's not. My husband knows it.
He's just banking on the fact he'll die while there's still work.

Italicized lines from: "Coal Miners Told to Keep Working During the Outbreak Despite Close
Quarters Damaged Lungs." www.msn.com/en-us/money/markets.

What I Found Surveying a Well Site in Greene County

A narrow house that had once been blue.

A torn-off condemnation notice near a dimly lit window.

A screen door, hanging open.

A yellowed newspaper clipping from 1989 celebrating someone's 50th anniversary. On the back was a half-panel of *Family Circus*, one of the ones with all the dashes running through but no one in frame to leave them behind.

An urn labeled "Poor Clyde."

An old piggy bank shaped like a basset hound that smelled like old bananas. Inside was $3.06 in change.

A couch with a bed pillow and neatly folded sheets on it.

A pair of green corduroy slippers, men's, lightly worn.

An old woman who yelled, as best she could, "what in the Lord's name are you doing in my house?"

"Jesus Christ," I said. "You about gave me a heart attack."

She brandished her cane at me, forcing me back against a teetering stack of books.

"Ma'am, I'm a contractor for Equitable. All this is condemned. The county is exercising eminent domain for the well. This—"

"The only thing that's condemned is the souls of those suits trying to kick me out. This is ancestral land!"

"—ma'am, this wasn't supposed to be occupied. Isn't."

"Ancestral land! The Kulmers have been here since Lincoln!"

"Here's a copy of the notice of condemnation," I said. "From the county. I'm going to take a look outside while you read it over. This house ain't safe for occupancy."

An upright piano, an old ornate one with the candle holders. When I hit the lowest key the hair on my arms stood up. I heard something scuttle around inside.

A 24-volume *Encyclopedia Britannica* with a mushroom growing out of volume 19, RAYN to SARR.

A purple sweatshirt, worn by the same old lady from before, with a print of Tweety Bird on it.

"Now look here," she said, advancing slowly toward me.

"Ma'am?"

"I been here since 1927 and they'll take me out of this place toes up. You tell your boss—"

"Ma'am, I'm afraid this isn't really negotiable. They're gonna have the dozer out here tomorrow to knock all this down. They was under the impression all these houses had been vacated and sent me to survey the site for demolition."

"—tell him to come down here and speak to me like a man if he's going to just go about knocking down people's homes."

A photo of a sour-looking man in black and white over top of a useless light switch in the stairwell.

"How in the hell you been living out here so long? Your power's out."

A queen bed that slumped in the middle, still made, with moss growing all over it. I could hear the old lady ranting and raving from the bottom of the stairs.

A closet full of mildewed church wear.

A Romeo y Julieta cigar that still smelled pretty good.

A cracked step. I heard it give from below.

"Ah! Crump's sake!"

The poor lady had slumped down, her corduroy slipper stuck.

"Shit," I said. She gave me a look of hatred and fright. I stepped over her into the room with the piano. "Ma'am, just hold still. I'm gonna pull you out."

"You keep your hands off me. Might as well let me stay in here."

"Hang tight, there, ma'am."

"Bulldoze me like you will my family, you devils."

"Okay, I'm gonna put an arm under you. Turn your foot now, real gentle."

She smelled like talc and cedar. I never understood how these rickety old people always smelled so fresh. You could sell a million Yankee Candles with the smell off my grandpa's cardigans, swear to God.

"And up we go," I said.

She looked even more hateful now that I'd helped her, but she was done ranting.

A fancy old German baptismal certificate.

A bloody sock.

"Mrs. Kulmer, I think it's best if I take you down to see a doctor. Your ankle's bleeding a lot. Them steps is probably a tetanus risk, if I'm being honest."

"I'm not going anywhere," she said, dripping blood on the ottoman.

"Goddammit," I said under my breath.

A little oil lamp, burning away with a fluttering sound.

Dozens, maybe hundreds of cans of food on a wire shelf.

A plate with half-eaten potted meat and some green beans.

Several ornate plates with Chinese-style paintings on them.

A small gold crucifix.

A photo of the old lady with her late husband, smiling in front of a green background. He wore a brown suit and looked a bit like my old man. I found the downstairs powder room and rummaged around in the cupboards.

Some gauze and antiseptic that had expired in '94. I took them back out to Mrs. Kulmer but she was breathing heavy on the couch.

"We got to get you down to town," I said. "I can help you to my truck."

An old wheelchair with flat tires and a fake blue leather seat. I lowered Mrs. Kulmer into it and wheeled her down to where I'd parked. Her face was crumpled in pain and her sock was soaked in blood.

"It ain't far," I said. "I'll go slow."

We snaked out past two more falling-down houses and onto the main road. It was quiet except for the distant hum of a train in the valley. I cracked the window. The air smelled like pine and sunshine.

"Beautiful country," I said.

She didn't say thank you when I dropped her off at the little urgent care by the Family Dollar. I stepped out for a smoke and called my boss. When I peeked through the window into the waiting room, they'd already taken her back.

Bright sunshine among little fluffy clouds.

A wooded hillside.

A sagging blue house that'd soon be a wastewater pond.

Mildred's Flight

Love was the airline ticket, a grown son in California,
And you walking the length of the cabin,

Its long columns of seats not the single row
You always arranged buried deep in the wings.

    67 years mistaking the view:
    The fearlessness you called up
    To expect the sleeping earth would
    Take leave at your feet, the clouds

    Shearing away from the swing
    Of your chairback, broad sky.
    You told me how children
    Ran into the street to catch

Sight of a plane, a stitch of silver above the Ohio
So rare in those days, and the Depression on,

And maybe that's why you waited so long
To leave us below, sure the X you saw up there

Was too thin crown to foot to hold more
Than one man aloft. But I'll hold you there,

Millie, marveling at what you can see of the wings,
The widows of the first class stored bravely inside.

On Broadway

She plays guitar on Broadway, an avenue in Pittsburgh,
a small-town affair, a clear early spring. The girl sits
on the stoop alongside the bakery, hardware store, bar,
twanging Chopin, she waits.

A man with dark curls walks into her sunlight.
He sits down beside her, they both know why he came.
Passing music and cigarettes back and forth between them,
their shoulders dipping and swaying in chaotic beats.

His chords slash, smooth vibrations, he's practiced
for decades, swell of storm on back roadways,
coyotes clamoring for prey. Her neck bristles
back arching, her blouse sticks to her ribcage,
They'll say she's too young, but it's already too late.

He strums and she listens before taking the lead,
her notes slide in new patterns, like cries in the rain,
the frets sizzle and drum, her fingertips splitting,
aching later for hours, a dull copper green.

Iva Allen-Dunlap

Shadyside, Ohio 1917-1985

whenever i see
vintage American cars or
hear about the GEM of Egypt,
apply red lipstick and rouge,
it's you who comes to mind.

you are the spirit
of all my summer vacations,
church fairs, comic book piles,
and hay rides over the cattle farm.

how you said people should pull
off the road and bow their heads
when a hearse goes by, and "in
your chimney of success, consider
me a brick."

i remember you driving a
gold '70 Chevy LS6 454, how
you'd stretch to reach the pedals,
describing earth stewardship and
countryside littering while we
cruised and i revved toward
the sound of getting here.

Ken

Ken was historical,
brazen, bold and serious about using his hands
to build 20' by 20" square log cabins in the middle of his front yard
right beside an astonishing pile of rusted metal scrap
that he said was harboring
a heavy, large black iron safe
with something inside it
about *Jesse James.*

His house clutters with skins,
skulls and stuffed animals
whose glass eyes follow you around
and instruments
he made—and
he makes sure we know this—
"made without instructions."
Everything is wood. All kinds.

He rattles on about his ex-wives
and shows us a petite replica of a two-seater
fashioned for them of cedar.
He shows us how
one toilet sits on top of the other and
winks—his eyes glowing.

He tells us he lived in Alaska most of his life
notable there for his craftsmanship.
There are pictures on the walls of him
in tan buckskin, hands on a rifle

and in front of a
two-story log cabin he built
near Tongass Forest.

He points to the pried open jaws of a shark on the wall
and tells us "a frame for a picture of my last wife"
and proceeds to tell us he served in World War II
"the great war" *he* calls it.

He now raises deer on his 150 acres and shoots bucks
for impotent Ohio hunters to carry bragging rights
with the casings he sells them too,
for their pockets.

The jeep he takes us in to inspect the cabin
on the back 40
in rural southwestern Ohio,
overheats and we walk the rest of the way.
He calls us "city slickers."
He thinks we have never roughed it.
We are tempted to buy the log cabin on his back 40,
not because of the scenery or
that we envision ourselves there,
but only because of Ken.

As we leave
he brings us out two cold pops
and yells as we pull away
"Next time you come,
bring a widow."

Workshop Comparing Chinese Zen Poetry to Appalachian Poetry

Inside
Poets write about nature.
Outside
Honeysuckle blooms,
Birds laugh,
Pine boughs nod in the wind,
Rain drops,
Fallen tree sinks into Mill Creek.

Inside
Poets read their poems to each other.
Outside
I drop this poem, like you, Li Po,
On the water,
Send it to the creek,
To the river,
To the bay,
To the sea,
To the sky,
To the cloud,
Where then, like you, Li Po,
It will fall down,
Come back
To sluice the wind,
Amuse the birds,
Glisten the pine,
Swell the creek,
Feed the honeysuckle,
And me.

Reparations

Being good isn't good enough
anymore. We gushed from heat
to this world covered in blood so
the expectations were small:

don't sink your teeth in another
child's flesh, a shoulder of your own
species. Play nice. When the wind
takes your diamond kite over the trees let

brother, sister or white
friend hold the string. You get
pretty good at it, the law's premise,
living peacefully among your own.

If you steal something just
give it back. Leave home.
Buy a salt box in the suburbs
so your parents can brag about you.

Make the city bigger, its powerful
population billowing over the empty
plains like golden grass, or the shuttle
launch's exhaust, which lifts us

into the Space Age. Can you believe
we've never made it past the moon
never put anyone on Mars? The best
we could do was television,

where we finally see it, long after
the moon dies and becomes the white
of an eye rolled back every night.
See our people sinking

knees into human flesh, into throats,
pumping the jacketed bullets in
bodies of black and brown, all
while we were being good.

I'm talking the end, tidal waves and
Santa Anna winds sweeping flames
from the murderous cars to
our back doors, Bermuda grass

and boxwoods. When the heat ignites
our wild hearts we want injustice obliterated but
it was never good enough just
being good. It takes more, being born

of the heat which destroys you and drives you
someplace dark as the richest soil
where buffalo lay after
our fathers slaughtered them.

It takes the blood
which fell enriching us and then
us giving it back.

Migration of a Native Tribe

perhaps from a razor blade
—Joseph Brodsky, "Elegy"

A close-up of the journey—
a cutting-edge of trail—
beard to whisker in union of—
after the fire of cannons
wherever we went—
the onward journey
deeper into the meaning of moving—
the moving of meaning.

Sonnet to the Pandemic in Southeastern Ohio

Pine needles like sticks of black feathers roost in the winter moon,
tall and unmoved by the cold. Smallmouth bass sink into the river
and thicken on the bone, suspended in the grey distance of water.
    Love
is the famine of rats. Grocery store checkouts are crammed with
    animals

who fear their lives without: milk, eggs, bread. Somewhere, snow
    trucks
start their engines and idle in parking lots far away—waiting. A fox
does not come out of the thicket nor a rabbit out of the hole; a
    possum mother,
her babies swinging from her teats, was once marsupial in the
    moonlight.

Snowflakes that drift over currents of empty twilight converge,
    pinnacles
of their crowns clustering in the air before settling on frozen
    ground.
Where a window is a box of light in the darkness, a man removes
    his clothes
and his watch and belt, and he decreases item by item until there is
    nothing left—

his lover, naked under the covers, pulls back the heat collected
    around her body
before he slides in beside her, grateful—their bodies dormant yet
    alive.

Layers

> *We get to have the same kinds of opportunities that our*
> *grandparents did, and that's something we never thought would*
> *happen.*
> *—Pennsylvanian working for the shale gas industry*
> *(energyindepth.org)*

This is not my land
to weep over.

This is what my neighbors say,
women at the market
and men in diners with relatives

tucked into the graveyard
on the hill opposite my porch.

If they want the neatly plotted
well pads, the drill rigs,
the heavy trucks that rut
and split asphalt
like year-round frost heaves,

if they want these things
and the cash they bring
for new dairy barns and duallies,

then I should just shut up.

Take my care elsewhere.

As the town turns cold
and gray, I leave
the porch but haunt
my windows.

The goldenrod dulled,
sumac burned out,
I peer into brown
shadows for deer staring
from their windows.

Every hardwood
overhead
is a scaffold
of bones;
every hawk
an angel.

And across
the valley,
the sun dives
deep into
beloved
gravestones,

names with
more claim
than me
to what lies miles below, pierced by fresh hopes, and shaken by the
    blasts.

SELF

From the Editor

Yours is a poem waiting,
like the narcissus in my yard, to bloom.
Poor little buds are getting fooled.
I'm afraid they may blossom just in time for Thursday's frost.
And that, as you know, will end their short lives!
So your beautiful start is about being fooled.
But for a moment the narcissus will flower,
brilliant enough to give all who look upon it
a fleeting taste of spring. Yes!
Being fooled is the star attraction
— and your first stanza sings!

I just returned from a long walk where I thought about you
and your poem and how much I enjoy hiking
through winter and, as winter becomes spring,
how easy it is to be fooled.
How we are so easily given to promise.
I thought, too, about how we waste our very best years
trying to create meaning, how we hope
to balance the poet's desire with the publisher's standard
and end up mired in identifying orphan lines
abandoned at the bottom of a page
or kerning the space between characters
where meaning is often lost. In fact, we are
the narcissus in the yard,
pushing up through the frozen earth.
When finally we do break through,
how little time we have!
We should be grateful, I suppose,

for resolute buds that manage against all odds
to come between ambition and discovery.
What is our calling, after all,
if not *to be astonished?*

Survival

When Paul suggested we go hunting, I just kept staring at the old photo of us all together at Clear Creek that one summer, must have been '95 or so judging by my bowl cut and Paul's crew, Ma's perm and pink top, a bottle of beer in Dad's hand as his other arm hung around all three of us. Most of the box had been photos of the men of my family hunched down in the snow beside dead deer, or holding gobblers upside down so their beards stuck out, or alongside a row of trout, squirrels, rabbits, pheasants, doves, ducks—you name it. But that photo and the day we took it stood out among the camo and the blaze orange. That same trip I shot a rifle for the first time. Excited from hitting the target on my first shot, I turned toward the rest of my family with a smile and the loaded .22 caliber still in my hand. The barrel pointed up, but that wasn't the point. A loaded gun stays pointed downrange. Dad took off his belt and hit me across the ass eight times, one for each bullet in the clip, but the real sting came when he asked if I thought I could live with myself after killing someone I loved.

Paul called my name and I looked up to see his ass sticking out from behind the open door of the gun cabinet. Already he sported camo pants, a folding knife sheathed at the belt and a black T-shirt untucked to hide the few pounds he'd put on around the waist since I last visited.

"Well, want to hunt for a few hours or not?" he asked. Maybe the sight of all those guns gave him the itch to put them to use.

"Now? It's almost 10:30. What kind of luck do you hope to find so late in the day?"

"If you don't want to come, I'll go myself." He backed out of the cabinet holding my .270 mountain rifle. I say my rifle because I used it for deer all throughout my childhood, and Dad always said it would go to me. With our Dad, you had to earn things for yourself, so the guns he bought for us when we were just boys still belonged to him even as we became men. But we both knew who he intended each rifle or shotgun or pistol to go to when this day came. And that one was mine.

"I didn't say no. I just don't have any gear."

"Take a look around," he told me. So I did. At Ma's request, we'd been sorting through Dad's storage room, filled with piles of knives and tools, mounds of old and new clothes, a stack of traps and a crate of half-full boxes of ammunition, just to name a few, and we'd only started after I'd finished breakfast twenty minutes ago. You could outfit an entire hunting party from this room alone. "None of it's any good to dad now," Paul added without emotion, just a cold, straight fact of life, "so why bother getting upset about it?" But I got a little upset about it.

"I don't have a spot."

"I've got your spot, little brother—Joy's place." Now Paul used that same smartass tone he'd perfected as a kid and carried into adulthood, a drawn-out accent that was half hillbilly and half 1840's prospector, the one that made his attempts at being annoying all the more annoying. "I been keepin' it warm for ya. James got his first doe there 'bout a week back."

The news caught me off guard, maybe because his son used my old spot or maybe because his son had already reached hunting age, though in our family you were old enough the day you were strong enough to drag a deer out of the woods with your father's tag around the ear claiming he shot it should anyone ask. I reminded him of all we needed to sort so we could claim it ourselves or give it away to our uncles or our cousins or our cousins' kids. He looked across the unsorted piles on the floor and said it could wait.

"Hunting can wait," I said.

As the words came out I knew I'd been away too long, drifted farther from home than I'd known. For me, hunting could wait; it had waited while I got my degree and it continued to wait while I spent my twenties looking for better jobs in better cities, drinking into those same dawn hours Paul spent in the woods, chasing women who had no intention of starting a family or settling down in the country and setting the alarm for four a.m. so I could go sit calmly in the woods and wait. Quickly I added, "till tomorrow. It's better in the morning." Paul just kept looking over the bolt and barrel of my .270 as if it were telling him secrets.

"Not with Joy's place. You know that apple tree's a night spot. And don't go saying you don't have a damn license because we can stop and get one on the way. Now, any more excuses?" I wasn't sure why I was resisting—it was a beautiful winter day for hunting and I hadn't even gone hiking in years. I should have wanted to go, and as I thought about it a moment, I did want to. Why the hell not? He was right—this could wait. "But hey," Paul went on, "if you don't have it in ya anymore, you can stay here sifting through boxes of old pictures."

There I sat, on an overturned bucket with a photo in my hand, surrounded by objects I didn't know what to do with, unable to remember why I'd started looking through the box of photos in the first place. I looked at our family one more time, stood up and held the photo out to Paul. "I'll trade you," I said. He took it, got lost in it for a moment the way I had. "Hey, I said trade, asshole. That's my gun you're holding."

He set the photo on the work bench beside him, patted me on the shoulder and handed me the rifle. My arm tensed against the weight and right away I noticed the dent I'd put in the stock the first year I joined my brother and father on a deer hunt. State Game Lands in the Alleghenies. Dad let us walk ahead to learn the way. Paul and I had been side by side, each gradually speeding up until we were racing to be the first to top the ridge. I had just pulled ahead when I slipped and the gun broke my fall. Again Dad took off his belt right there in the woods and lashed it across my bare ass for being irresponsible with his rifle. When Dad told me to bend over, Paul started laughing in that same obnoxious voice before Dad told him he'd get the same unless he shut up, and I watched Paul's expression change as my face showed the pain that could have just as easily gone to him. When we dropped Paul off at his spot for the day, my brother offered me his sitting cushion as an extra support for my sore ass. Dad had half a grin on his face as I took it, but a second later he was already heading deeper into the forest.

I had to run just to catch up.

* * *

My father's clothes came together on me.

The camo parka he bought for his own father and kept after he died, the hat with ear flaps that I later traded for a normal stocking cap, the gloves with the trigger finger cut off, the blaze orange vest with the pockets and the pouch in the back for rabbits or squirrels. Just like Dad had done when I was young, Paul started rattling off a list of things I'd need and throwing gear at me without looking to see if I'd caught it. It all fit just fine, except that the biggest pair of boots Dad owned barely squeezed on and needed to be wrestled off by Paul as I held onto the work bench. I said I could deal with the tight fit for the day, but Paul reminded me that we could grab a new pair when we stopped for my license, that a good pair of boots never gets old. So I left Dad's storeroom in full hunter's regalia except for my black dress shoes, the ones I'd been wearing when I'd gotten the call the day before last and in a daze threw some stuff in a suitcase before heading to the airport. Just like then, I had the feeling I was forgetting something.

Before we left, we stepped into the kitchen where Ma sat smoking and watching TV. She had been crying, of course, and hearing about her boys heading out to the woods, "in honor of their father" as she put it, brought on a new wave of tears and tissues. I felt guilty leaving her alone, but Paul was eager to get out the door. There was no point in asking if she wanted us to stay with her, but I asked anyway. Ma didn't hunt, but she always imagined the woods as a place where her boys could bond and become the kind of men she'd grown up around, the kind she'd married. Nothing would make her happier than for her two sons to spend the day in the woods together, and she told us so. "He'd be proud of you both," she added as we left. But I couldn't tell if this was the truth or just one of those things people say when someone's father dies.

* * *

The ride to the hunting spot always spoke to me, even if none of us in the truck said a word, just listened to country radio or the sound of tires kicking gravel from the road like rain against the truck bottom. It might have been the thrill of being young, how adult I felt getting to come along, how calm the world seemed before the sunrise. Or the contrasts—the warmth of the truck cab and the cold rushing through a crack in Dad's window, moving before a day of sitting still, high beams lighting up the dirt road ahead and the dark, dewy fields or forest floors just beyond the light's reach.

Scanning the passing fields for game was a family tradition, one way we trained our eyes. But that late morning I saw only the past—openings in the forest where turkeys used to gather, deer decoys next to swing sets, the same run-down porches and junked cars. Just before you merge onto State Route 426 there's a wide swath of grass cut through the hillside for power lines. One fall, when it was just me and Dad for some reason, we spotted a flock of turkeys there while driving past, and Dad pulled over, gave me my shotgun, and told me to creep up there and scatter the flock so I could practice calling them back together. He knew damn well I had no chance of getting close enough in such open woods. I knew this too, but took it as a test, avoided each stick so that the only sound I made was the soft crunch of dead leaves. About seventy yards away from the flock I looked up and saw them scuttling away. So I bolted, ran as fast as I could, jumped a log and burst into the clearing screaming like a madman, hoping to put the fear of God so deep in their turkey hearts that they wouldn't know which way to turn. But they stayed together. I could hear Dad howling with laughter as I walked back to the truck. Closer, I saw his face was bright red and there were tears in his eyes. He told the story to the hicks at the bar that night while I messed around on the pool table, told it a hundred times since. And I heard something in his voice each time he'd tell it, a tone I knew I'd miss.

Paul and I talked about the unusual December warmth and how some snow would be better for spotting deer, our arms resting on our rolled-down windows just like our younger, cooler selves. The radio played country music, the new stuff I couldn't stand, basically pop and the worst kind of it, but there were a few times an oldie took me back to growing up, and I'd look over at Paul to see if the memories hit him too. He'd just stare ahead or look to a field as it passed. I wanted to tell him I hadn't forgotten the classics, that I'd took that part of growing up on the road with me, that I sometimes stayed up late getting drunk alone so I could look them up on YouTube and sing along.

Then a song we knew well came on. He must have felt my eyes on him the whole time because without turning he asked, "something on your mind?" There was. One certain line in the song took me back to that same family vacation from the photo. Dad couldn't understand the lyric, so he just mumbled it, and there was something in the air at that moment that drove us all to an insane laughter over it. We spent the rest of the trip imitating him, and he would just mumble along the same way, glad to make the family laugh. So, when the lyric came on I copied Dad's mumble. Paul turned like he was about to ask what the hell I was talking about. Then I saw him remember and start to laugh. He'd probably listened to that song a thousand times as an adult and never heard Dad's voice the way I did. And as we sang along together, he became the young Paul I remembered from that trip, and like a revelation I noticed Paul's goofy, intentionally-irritating voice had a little of Dad's in it.

After it finished, he repeated Ma's description of Dad's warbling—"like a cat clawing its ears off."

"She was right. Dad couldn't sing worth a damn."

"He sure tried though."

"Couldn't remember a lyric either."

"Didn't give a shit! Made 'em up that whole trip to Cook's Forest and the way back."

"That time was Clear Creek," I said, because it was. "The Cooks Forest trip came later."

"Bullshit. I remember exactly. Cook's Forest—that was the same trip I crept within thirty yards of that albino fawn with the camcorder. Still got the video somewhere to prove it. Only albino I ever recorded."

"I don't doubt that, but a video of a white deer doesn't prove what happened the rest of the trip. The time with the singing was the year before. Remember the picture —"

"Fine, you're right. You're always fucking right! Why can't you just shut the fuck up and listen every once and a while?"

We both grew quiet. A group of bikers came upon us then. Their engines became one and, for a moment, drowned out the world.

* * *

I only once asked Dad what he thought about animal rights and the ethics of hunting. I must have been about thirteen or so. We were walking up the same hill I saw again as Paul and I pulled into Joy's lot. He kept walking ahead and after a while I assumed he hadn't heard me, so I called his name and he turned. "Who told you that shit?" he asked, and before I could answer he turned and kept walking. A minute or so later he started telling me about how the population of deer needed regulating, or they'd starve or eat all the crops and screw over the farmers, or die out on the highway where they might take some driver along with them. He got more excited as he went on, saying he'd like to know how many vegetarians ever tried to raise six kids on poverty wages the way his father had. And oh, didn't animals eat other animals? And plants were alive too, weren't they? What made us so high and mighty to fuck up the natural order of things?

I'd heard it all before, eavesdropping on conversations between my uncles, reading through their hunting magazine and pamphlets. He seemed to have made his point and we climbed the rest of the ridge in silence.

But when we reached the top, he stopped again and turned to me. "But it's important you know that all of that—true as it is—it's not the whole story." Dad always spoke without thinking, but now he seemed to dig for the right words. "Death's as much a part of life as anything. No real tragedy in it, no more than, say, the sun going down on a nice day. You wish it could go on forever, but it can't. The real tragedy is people forget that. They get comfortable thinking life's never got to end, then, sooner or later, they get a harsh reminder it does, and sometimes they can't take it, and they fall apart." He shifted his shotgun to his left hand and put his right on my shoulder. "Your granddad used to say there's something spiritual about choosing to be part of it, the living and the dying I mean. You give up that part of yourself who'd rather not face it, or pretend we're above it, who'd die never having given a thought to what their fathers did to survive." He spat on the ground and looked back down the hill. "You know the rituals in church, right? How they remind us the way Jesus died so we could all survive? Well killing a deer, you can focus on what dies or what survives. Take the meat home, feed your family, teach your kids how to do the same. That's hunting for me, remembering what surviving looks like. But you're right, we've got a choice now. And you'll have to make your own."

He was dodging the question, at least that's what I thought at the time, what I thought for years after as I moved around and met new types of people who asked me that same question when I told them about my past, who watched me struggle to explain something. Eventually, I stopped trying.

As we finished the drive and pulled into Joy's that day, I kept thinking about those words, how some people fall apart, and kept replaying in my mind the plane ride here, how I started thinking about Dad being gone, really gone, and how I felt myself starting to fall apart in front of everyone on the plane, how I ran to the bathroom and locked myself in, cried like a baby, for fifteen minutes, alone, far above the Earth, even wishing the plane would fall from the sky. Then I looked at Paul as he drove his truck to his favorite hunting spot, strong as he'd ever been, on the outside at least, and I wondered if Dad had told him the same thing—if the hardened, vacant expression I now saw on his face was what surviving looked like.

* * *

Joy had kept a farmhouse by herself since her husband died about fifteen years back. She had two boys who were grown and lived off in cities somewhere with families of their own. Dad had met Joy in the simplest way a hunter can meet a landowner—he scouted the field from his truck and one day he walked up on her porch, knocked on the door, asked how much land she owned and then for permission to hunt there. I once asked Dad how he got people to say yes and he said they didn't always, in which case he'd thank them and move on to the next place. But he always agreed to play by the landowner's rules or not at all, and he always offered part of the meat as payment. If the meat part didn't work out, he'd still drop off a bottle of her favorite whiskey or an extra turkey around Christmas. When we stopped at the supercenter for my license earlier that day, Paul had bought the biggest bird in the store.

Joy's two labs—one chocolate and the other yellow—ran out to greet us as we pulled in. I thought they'd run right under the truck until Paul yelled some mumbled command similar to "g'on 'n get!" and they ran off into the field, nipping and biting after each other in unfinished circles, testing each other's strength. We parked, grabbed the turkey and headed to the house.

Joy invited us in, thanked us about five times in three minutes for the turkey and offered to make coffee or cut us a slice of pie. I said I'd love some pie. Paul refused. As I sat and Joy dug through the fridge, Paul told me to hurry up and eat fast so we could set up in time, even though he'd said earlier that we had plenty of time. It wasn't long before I learned why. Over the next five minutes, Joy managed to bring up everything about Dad that Paul and I were avoiding—how much she would miss him, how nice the funeral would be, all the gifts he used to bring her, the first half of some racy story about Dad drunk at a party years back. She wasn't sobbing or anything, and there was no change in her voice—this was a woman who kept up a farmhouse with just a pair of dogs—but her eyes got a bit watery, and so did mine. But Paul, he had his back turned most of the time, staring out the window at that old ridge he longed to climb.

* * *

"I was thinking I'd put you in the apple tree and I'll take Dad's spot further up the ridge."

Paul walked beside me as we topped the ridge and stopped to catch our breaths while looking down on Joy's farmhouse and the hills beyond. I recognized his tone well, not his but Dad's or our grandfather's, the way men in my family talked to the friends-of-friends that would sometimes tag along, weekend-warrior types who needed someone to take charge and tell them what to do on a hunt. And now I was along for Paul's ride, no different I guessed from his son the week before.

"I'll take Dad's spot," I offered, innocently enough.

"You even remember where it is?" He had a point. Dad had always dropped me off at the apple tree and went on alone. At dusk he'd reemerge and we'd walk out together. I think I'd only seen his spot once while scouting together. I'd be lucky to find it by myself.

"I'll manage. You take the apple tree."

"What are you, some type of idiot?" Paul didn't mean offense here— this was just the way we talked to each other. "The apple tree's easily the better spot. James already claimed my doe tag, plus I got all post-season to come up here and try out Dad's muzzleloader. I want to save my tag. You might not get another shot before you leave town. You wanna kill something or not?"

Maybe that was it. I wasn't sure I wanted to. This was my heritage, my family tradition, something I'd taken pride in years back. And I wasn't sure I cared anymore. I was just along for the ride.

* * *

Once you're set up, there's not much to do but listen, look and think. Once I'd set up in the apple tree I decided to do as much of the first two as possible. I once asked Dad if it was okay to think or daydream in the woods, and he said you couldn't help but think but that you should try to focus on where you were, not where you had come from or where you wish you could be. Now I wondered what he thought about during all those times he sat here, looking and listening, if his mind ever kept running back down the hill to the world he left behind, to his problems, his worries, or off into fantasy, maybe that life as a hunting guide he'd always dreamed of, quitting the machine shop before Paul was born and moving to a real mountain range. Or maybe he often found the kind of peace I imagined, just listened to the breeze, his eyes following tall grass as it swayed, smelling the rotted winter leaves, the hair on the back of his neck burrowing into the bark of this same tree behind me.

With no wind to sway the trees, a stillness fell upon the forest that froze time, and for an hour nothing moved. I was thinking about thinking about nothing when a squirrel came down from a tree about fifty yards away and ran along the top of a log, pausing every few feet. I put my scope up for a closer look, remembered how hard it can be to find what you're looking for. The squirrel crossed to the far side of a tree. I spent ten minutes trained on that tree waiting for him to circle back around. He never did.

My ass started to hurt and I wanted to go home. So goes the normal progression of thoughts while hunting. I convinced myself I'd see no deer, that it was too late in the day, that they'd all gone off somewhere together, maybe to the fields, maybe to the bar for drinks. I imagined deer sitting around a poker table, telling stories the way the old men used to when they played cards back at our camp when I was young. I checked my watch. I thought about resting my eyes—I hadn't slept much lately—but was kept awake by the image of Dad telling me to keep on my guard. I decided to try clearing my mind again, and eventually I got close to not thinking, just enjoying the still of the forest. The sun peaked through the wintry haze above on its way down, and I realized it was getting dark and that soon it would be time to go home. But I hadn't seen anything yet, and so now I didn't want to go home anymore, not without a story to tell. Paul would ask, Ma would ask, at the funeral people would ask, and I when I told them all I had seen was a squirrel, they'd laugh or shrug and say oh well, that's the way it goes before walking off disappointed. So even though my ass still hurt and my mind kept racing, I started to wish the sun wouldn't set so quickly, that the day could give me a few more hours and the hope of something crossing my path. So goes the normal progression of thoughts while hunting.

Then I heard something, started scanning the forest's openings and saw three deer moving along the hillside in my direction, just over a hundred yards away. They looked like the brown shadows of skinny dogs from that distance, appearing between trees and stopping to feed or waste time like deer do. Almost instinctively I began to swing the gun inch by inch in their direction. They weren't running, so I could wait for a decent shot. Through the scope I saw only trees until finally I picked out the figure of the first, then the second, both doe, and then the buck, three points on one side. That meant he was legal, and if I followed Dad's advice I would shoot right now that I had him in my sights. With a rifle, Dad always said, take the first shot you get, because you might not get another. We watch deer in the off season. When it's hunting season, we shoot.

But Dad was dead now, and I didn't want to rush the shot. I watched the buck follow slowly behind the doe until they reached a small opening. This part here, the voyeurism, the waiting, the connection between hunter and prey where you held that life in your finger—this was it for me, the part I could never explain to friends who'd never hunted, who saw no sport in what my family did. To them, the deer was helpless and pulling the trigger was easy, like flipping some kind of death switch. You just needed to want to kill, that was all. But it's not that way at all. It's more like a free-throw or an at-bat or a fourth-down that's going to decide a whole game or an entire season. Hours, days, weeks come down to one shot. And even the best can miss.

I found the buck's kill zone in my sights.

And I thought back to Dad's words about hunting, about some people not wanting to face death, about survival. And I remembered him next to me, whispering in my ear to ease the safety off, to let out a breath and squeeze, and how then he grew silent and waited, waited to see what I could do. And I felt like he was next to me then, holding that same silence, waiting to see what I would do, just like his father had done for him.

The deer looked up. It was the only time in my life I felt like the dead were watching me.

I felt their breath on my face as I squeezed.

* * *

Ten minutes later it was near dark and I saw a faint silhouette walking toward me. I had climbed down from my spot and waited there after the deer had run off. Of course, Paul heard the shot, and when he asked I told him I didn't know if I'd hit the deer or not. He rolled his eyes and I flipped him off. We took out our flashlights and went to have a look.

I pointed out the general area where the deer had stood and was ready to admit I couldn't shoot worth shit after five minutes of looking for blood. It had been a long shot, sort of, and I was out of practice shooting, and I could always lie and say the deer was running. Embarrassment started to creep in. I imagined those conversations at the funeral, having the one story worse than not seeing anything at all. Then Paul spotted a blood trail, faint but it led the right way. His face lit up.

"You got him brother!" he hollered, his arm around me. "See that bubble in the blood there? That means you at least one-lunged him. He's down for the count somewhere close, guaranteed."

As we followed the trail my mind went back to a conversation I'd had with Paul when we were barely teenagers. We'd been following Dad single file through the woods on our way back to the truck, each of us dragging our deer through the snow, taking turns smoothing out a trail and stopping to rest every couple hundred yards while Dad walked ahead, stopping but not backtracking to join us. He was letting us have the experience to ourselves. Paul asked me if I would rather have a deer fall down dead right away or have to track it.

"You some kind of idiot?" I remember I had said. "Fall down dead right away. Why would you wanna risk not finding it?"

"Cause tracking a deer is more exciting." He was catching his breath. We both were. "What about if you were the deer?"

"If I was the deer, I'd want you to miss."

Paul ignored me. "I think I'd want to have that last run."

"In crazy pain?"

"Maybe, but at least you'd get to know what was happening. You wouldn't just wake up in heaven with no chance to, you know, see what it was like."

"What what's like?" I asked. But then it hit me what he meant, and he never bothered to clarify, and we both just let it go, went back to dragging our deer through the snow.

Now Paul and I came to a spot where the blood trail stopped. No deer. I asked what to do next. "We'll spread out and see if we can pick it back up." He panned his flashlight around the area. I looked up and saw a sky turned dark blue, stars already coming into view as the night came on. "If we can't find it we'll mark this spot and come back at first light. He's here somewhere though. This happens sometimes—you lose the trail just before you find the deer. Then you'll find a big spot of blood and the deer a few yards up from it. Not sure why. An old man I know thinks it's because they feel the end coming and try to outrun it, make one last lunge away from it, and they go so fast the blood stops flowing as they go. Then it catches up to them and that's it. They stop, accept it, find the first comfy spot and bed down. Crazy, huh? Not sure I buy it, but not sure how else to explain it. Guess I should look it up sometime."

Ma had been lying in bed with Dad when his heart gave out. She said all in all it took only a minute from the time she thought something was wrong to the time she knew he was gone. His eyes became huge and he looked like he wanted to say something but couldn't. She kept talking to him, asking if he was okay, but he couldn't hear her. He just kept looking up, trying to speak. I can imagine her asking, pleading to be told what to do, how to make it all better. But there was nothing to be done. Then she said she felt him go, and that was it.

Five minutes later I found a big spot of blood, just as Paul had said, and when I scanned the area with my flashlight I saw the buck just a few yards up. I might have tripped over him if I'd come from the other way. Seven points total, its body a bit smaller than I had thought. I hollered and Paul came running, put his arm around my shoulder. "You still got it, brother," he said. He looked me right in the eyes and I felt young again. "Remember how to gut him?" he asked.

"Damn sure I don't."

"Well I can clean him if you want. It's your ass dragging him out of here anyway." He moved for his knife and it occurred to me what I'd forgotten at the house—Dad's pocket knife. I could picture it home on the work bench, right next to his compass and the rusty water canteen our grandfather had used in the war.

"No," I said, "it'll come back to me. Just hold the light and let me borrow your knife—I left Dad's at home."

"That's your knife now if you want it." I was already on my knees, and when I turned back I saw him holding out his knife, still folded. "But for now, I've got you covered."

I poked the deer with my rifle to check, but clearly it was dead. I handed the rifle to Paul and slid in closer, ran my hand along the white of its stomach, felt the fur, even pet the thing. I had no desire to gut it. What I wanted at that moment was to ask Paul what he thought Dad had been trying to say to Ma the instant before he died. As I knelt there, running my fingers through the fur, I imagined each possible reaction. Maybe Paul would get angry I'd asked, hint that I'd ruined the moment like on the ride here. Maybe he'd finally give it a long, deep thought and let a tear escape from the corner of his eye. Maybe he'd put his hand on my shoulder and, in a voice more Dad's than his own, tell me that it didn't matter, that everything he needed to say had been understood long ago by any of us who took the time to know him, who took the time to quiet our minds, listen to the forest, and hear what it had to say.

I opened my brother's blade. As I slid it past the fur, through the skin and up along the stomach, the warm blood that struck my hand and the putrid smell of death overpowered my senses, turned my stomach, made me want to vomit. And I knew there was only one way to put a stop to it.

I took a deep breath and did what needed to be done.

Things You Can Only See If You're Not Looking

A lark's condensed breath
As it sings a too-cool morning into day

The star next to the star
You think is Alnilam
Sparkling in The Hunter's belt
Low in the November sky

Your lover's hand reaching
Just before it touches your shoulder

Ghost cats

The infinite grace
Of the first raindrop

Green knowing it will be yellow
In February forsythia

Owls at night

Mars winking
Jupiter too
And Saturn
Venus with both eyes

The corpse's smile
Just before you pass

The tear you never cried

Yahoes in the canopy
Just after the limb to limb leap

The last pin oak leaf as it falls
The soundwave it makes

Squirrels in a beech grove

The bend in the tail of the comet

The animal nobody has ever seen

Sleep

The first purple redbud

The rise of trout downstream from your cast

Cedar Waxwings eating the last cherries

The color of the devil's eye

You mother's last breath

The spirit rising from everything
From you
From the river
From the grass blade and the elk
From the sentient wolf
And the sheep in the pasture
From hay in the field
From peaches in the orchard
From turtles in the pond

The swell and pull of it all
Lifting, lifting, lifting

What is Left Behind

The shelves are empty again, picked clean
like sinew stripped from bone, nothing left
but marrow and dust.
We cough pleas
into wind, pray they land in mouths
of strangers who recognize the taste
of hope and desperation.
We cough joy
into fists, unable to peel our fingers
from palm, the soft tips warmed
against callous and pulse.
We cough whispers
into the ears of our mothers, hope they fit snug
and turn to screams,
so the lullabies they gave
us never leave them.
We cough inheritance
into lessons we teach our children,
promise them we are different, teach them
that they are different.
We cough memory
into masks that block breath from escaping,
inhale to taste one last time the recipes
from our childhood table.
We cough splintered words
through head and heart. They shatter
like bone, the only pieces
we can attach ourselves to.

Every Person Deserves a Statue and Every Statue Deserves a Sledgehammer

After watching Ghost Busters *and hearing about Heather Heyer on the same day.*

The Twin Towers still stand,
and when two other buildings explode,
only fake rock hits the ground.
Everyone escapes.
No one has to jump.

And after the great eruption
of blimp-sized Mr. Stay Puft,
globs of gooey marshmallow
coat the city, the sidewalk, the people.
No dust. No ashes.
No one ever dies.

We were so foolish
to believe even for a moment
that ghosts could be busted,
to believe spirits lived
out there and not inside.

* * * *

Statues are ghosts
turned into marble,
saints easy to sledgehammer
compared to real ghosts,

like Robert E.
with his once-brown eyes

and once-trimmed beard
sleeping under the stars
of the Confederate flag
all across the South
and North and East and West.

We will never bust that ghost.
He lives on in each of us

just like Booker T. & Malcolm X &
Garret A. Morgan, inventor
of that other hood, the smoke hood,
predecessor to the gas mask,

just like Heather Heyer
gone to Charlottesville
to say Robert E. is no
greater or lesser than any of us,

to say, "If you're not outraged,
you're not paying attention,"

to ask, now that I too
am a ghost,
where is my statue?

* * * *

And that song from the movie
that worms inside
to play on and on and on—
"Who ya gonna call?"—

I dialed the number,
the line is dead.

Elegy at One Hundred and Thirty-Seven Feet

Sitting on top of your exclamation point, the Bicentennial Tower, I can see all of you. I see the city and the bay, the bustle and the calm, the past and the present. The top of the tower is empty today. There was an older couple when I first got up here, but they left after a few minutes. A seagull flew by before it landed on the slushy waters of the bay. I am in complete solitude in the middle of your busiest street. It's just you and me up here. Which is perfect, because it's about time we talked.

You have to leave. You know that, right? I understand all that's on your mind, but this isn't the future. This isn't your future. It certainly can be if you want, but you know how the rest of your life plays out if you choose that path. You'll take the first job offered to you after graduation. You can buy a moderately- priced home, probably close to the same neighborhood as your parents. Not that there's anything wrong with that; it's a nice neighborhood. Doors-unlocked-type neighborhood. Work your way into middle manage- ment, or whatever the plateau of your career is. If you choose this path, you settle. You stay safe.

The first thing I do on top of the tower is take a slow walk all the way around the observation deck. I forget how beautiful you are sometimes. The website said the tower is open every day, weather permitting. The weather certainly permitted today. It's deceptively cold, and I suppose being this high up and right on the water doesn't help, but the sun is out. Beaming, really. It makes your water sparkle, and your buildings glimmer. You're picturesque today. If I had to sell someone on you, today would be the day I'd do it. I look out over your water and see a woman walking her dog along the paths of Presque Isle. Days like this, you really bring the best out of your inhabitants.

You want the best for yourself, right? Settling isn't what's best for you. There is a whole world of possibility, how could you be so naive to think that what's best for you is here? That's intentional ignorance. Ignorance out of fear. Fear makes for bad decision making. Besides, it's not like you have to leave tomorrow. You just need to accept this decision in your brain, when the time comes. How many of the people who changed the world did so by staying put? Name one great person who sat idle and watched the world go by? How many of your idols stayed in the same place their whole lives?

I met you as soon as I came into this world. Looking south from on top of the tower, I can see the hospital where I was born. My parents work in that hospital and have longer than I've been alive, therefore, I suppose I owe that hospital more than I can actually articulate. My house, the food I eat, the memories of childhood vacations. I see the rest of your skyline, too. The hospital, the financial building, the marina, State Street and the Bayfront Connector. I've seen your buildings and walked your streets thousands and thousands of times, each creating new stories and feelings. Baseball and hockey games, theatre and comedy. Stores and bars, restaurants and colleges. All can be seen from this vantage point. You give more than you take.

It takes your soul and sucks it out of you, like a vacuum. Or a tar pit. Yeah, a tar pit is better. Because that's what this place is. You get stuck here. Can't move. Can't fight it. Until you give up. Look around at all the others stuck in the tar pit and get used to their faces, because those are the same faces you'll see over and over again. Every social outing. Movies, baseball games, bars, always the same faces. Every. Single. Time. Because this place is a god-damn tar pit. La Brea Erie. And you my friend, you're one foot in. Be careful where your next step leads you.

I take a few steps to the west. I can see parts of the Frontier neighborhood from here. When I was a kid, I used to walk the dog there. Of course, you already knew that. Those houses are so beautiful, so elegant. I don't know how you planned that one, but you sure got it right. I always imagined that would be where I lived when I grew up. A house on a tree-lined street, with a big backyard. Wife, kids, dog. During the summers, my house would be the place to be. Eating barbeque and drinking a little too much. Sitting around the fire until the sun goes down and the fireflies start making their presence known. Fall would arrive and my house would host holidays, Thanksgiving and Christmas, because I've got more than enough space for everyone to stay. All my friends and family around, all of us enjoying how kind you've been to us.

Six percent unemployment rate here. That's fifty percent higher than the rate of the whole state. Let that sink in. You know what that sounds like? That sounds like you're working a job you hate because you're not going to find one you love. Not here. Those jobs are few and far between here. Remember when you were a kid, and you would walk the dog in Frontier? That one house, the white one with the long brick driveway that overlooked the water? If you think you could ever afford that with the career opportunities here, you're fooling yourself. You're not a fool, are you? Look, I don't want to be a total downer, I'm just a realist. The beautiful life you pictured for yourself, it's still out there, trust me. But it's out there*, you get what I'm saying? This is a shit-town. And manure might be good for growing flowers, but those flowers always get picked so they can be delivered to a new destination.*

This destination, I don't know why I picked it to talk to you. Come to think about it, I've driven past this tower thousands of times and this is only the second time I've ever been in it. I came here once with my grandmother when I was maybe ten or eleven. When I look back to the west, I can see my grandmother's neighborhood. The working-class houses that used to make up your identity, now many of them are abandoned or condemned. How did you get like this? When did this happen? I don't remember you being this bad when I was growing up, but maybe I just wasn't able to notice then. Now you've become violent and dangerous, you've got a bad reputation. That is, if people have ever heard of you at all. Admittedly, I always wished I was from a bigger city. New York or Chicago or, hell, even Cleveland. Just somewhere everyone knows. Somewhere that brings some clout with it. You don't have clout. You aren't well known. You are just you.

You want to create your own identity, right? You're going to get lost in the identity of this city. You're going to get lumped in with all those who never left. The identity here is getting worse anyway. This place is starting to eat itself alive. Look around; you know it's true. You watch the news. Night after night it's murders and drugs and arrests. It's bad. How do you expect a place like this to embrace you? I know you love it, but it cannot love you back. No matter how much you wish it could. You won't be appreciated here. Places like this can't appreciate simple things like schools and jobs, how could they appreciate you? Your name won't be immortalized here. It can always be part of the past, but it can never be part of the future. It was never in the cards. It can be a fun fact for the cocktail parties and rooftop soirees that await you. Don't mourn it, because it certainly won't mourn you.

I've been sitting on top of the tower for almost an hour now, and while you are beautiful, I have other things to do today. I tap my pocket, as always, just to double-check my keys are there. They are, so I make my way to leave. The door to the observation deck is on the northern side of the tower, and before I enter the staircase, I look out over your water again. This is the only side I cannot see you from. Only your lake, which stretches until it meets the horizon. There is a large ship out there making its way to some unknown destination. I wonder where that ship started its journey, and I wonder where it is going. I wonder if that ship ever wishes it could just stay on the journey, and never have to arrive. It has to arrive, I know. But just for the moment, that ship and I can both look out and appreciate the beauty that you, Erie, have given us.

Epilogue

It has been nearly two years since I wrote this essay. At the time, I was already thinking about graduate programs all over the country and ranking and re-ranking the schools I wanted to go to in my head. Part of that was simply just how my brain is wired: I like to be prepared, even if I was two years away from even sending out applications.

Most of that, however, was because I was feeling very small at that point in time. Erie was small. Edinboro was small. I was small. Small people are never the people that go down in history. They don't change the world or have buildings named after them. They rarely even have their own Wikipedia page.

I was very fortunate to grow up in a house that always encouraged me to dream ambitiously. That with hard work and focus, I could achieve all that I could dream for myself. When I wrote this essay, I was doing just that. The problem that dreaming poses is that it can make us lose sight of what is directly in front of us. Or, perhaps worse, stop appreciating what we have.

The ambitious dream I had was to become Wright Thompson. When I joined the writing program, I told Dr. Carden the very first time I met her that I wanted to be a sportswriter. I would've given anything to be a features writer for *Sports Illustrated* or ESPN *The Magazine*, but I knew that was still far off into the future. I did everything I could to try to prove to myself that I was the best writer not just at Edinboro, not just the best writer in the state, but that I was the best damn writer in the country other than Mr. Thompson.

The problem was, I still felt small. I still felt stuck in a city that was both my own and not mine at all. I still felt that the future could not have come fast enough. I would often think to myself how I couldn't wait to move to whatever future city (most of which I had never even been to) would become my new home.

Then, all at once, the world came to a complete halt. A pandemic forced the end of my junior year to take place online. A summer of social justice marches shifted my priorities. The most important election of my lifetime, one that would shape America's place in the world, was teeing off. And, all at once, I didn't feel small anymore.

Before I had a chance to ever apply to any of these graduate schools I had long dreamed of, I decided that writing wasn't my path forward. Instead, after a long time of soul searching, and several long talks with my family, I realized that law was my way forward. I thought that I wanted to be the name in the byline, but instead came to realize I wanted to be the subject of the article.

Suddenly, the future seemed clearer than ever to me. I want to be the person who can make an actual change in the world. And change in the world starts with change at home. Instead of being the person who cannot wait to leave Erie, I instead find myself committed to being the person who can bring change to the city that is my home.

However, in almost a cruel twist of fate, now that I have accepted that I love this city, I have to leave it to go to law school. All that time spent wishing I could be anywhere else, and now, I will be, come fall. All that time wishing to be away from my family, and to make new friends, and now that it is real, I find myself hoping to speed up the future once again, to a time I can return home.

What I have learned over the last four years, the biggest and best lesson that Edinboro has given me, is to appreciate the journey. When I started here, I wanted nothing more than to be done. Get my diploma and get out. Now that the end is in sight, I find myself wishing I could slow down and take it all in. Take the time to click snapshots in my head, paint mental pictures, savor all of these moments because once they are gone, they are gone. *The Great Gatsby* teaches us that we can never recreate the past, which is why we must indulge ourselves in the present.

So, I will appreciate the journey.

I once again find myself dreaming ambitiously. The next three years will be very hard, but as a great American once said, "We choose to go to the moon, and do the other things, not because they are easy, but because they are hard." *Because they are hard.* Over the next three years, and every year after that, I will do the hard work. Because that is the only way to achieve our wildest dreams and make the change in the world we believe is worth making.

There will be times, surely, that it is too much. Completely overwhelming. I know, at least once, I will question my path in life. And, in these times, I will smile and remember this essay. I'll remember a time when I was ready to leave my hometown because I couldn't appreciate what it meant to me. A time when I was focused on greener pastures, not realizing I was making terrific friendships and meeting mentors who would shape my view of the world. A time that I couldn't possibly have imagined ever thinking of Erie fondly, or even yearning to go back. So, in these times, I'll smile. Then I'll go back to doing the hard work.

Where Lottie Lived

Over the years, neighbors offered to buy Old Lottie Burns's house. She always said no. She'd die first before she'd ever let someone live in that house.

"What's her story?" she'd overheard people asking each other. Walking their dogs, they'd peer into her windows, checking to see if Lottie was still there. Never stopped to have a conversation with her, offer her a chance to tell her stories of the house.

She figured they just hoped to catch a glimpse of her long white hair, to see how bent she was, how she had to walk with her hands locked behind her, how she had to stare forever to the floor or the ground. At night kids corned her doors, soaped her windows, singing, "Lottie, Lottie, got a sweet body, drinks hot toddies, eats from her potty."

She ached to show them how beautifully she could sing, to tell them her father had cried once when she sang "Ave Maria."

After her father died, her mother and her priest had said, "Just let's hold onto the *good* memories. That's all we can do." And for the most part, she had.

Still, it was too much, this staying in the house alone. Too much to keep up. When her mother had finally passed—taking with her all the chances she had to say she was sorry, to explain why she'd turned her eyes away—Lottie allowed the house to rot. It didn't take long for skunks to make a home in the cellar, babies and all. Mice tenanted, gnawing sundry antechambers the length of the foundation.

One night she awakened to her father's words, "Damn hard-headed, you are." His voice had broken in. So she closed off those rooms where his sounds breathed from the switch-plates, where his scent lingered in the floorboard knots. She no longer cared to cover with framed photos the plaster dents where the dog was slammed or where her skull connected. She took the frames down, picked at the wall's chalky pieces, let them fall to the floor.

Years passed and The Blessed Mother statue continued to heave from the ground roots, listing away from the house. A missing nose. Her blue gown chipped, mottled. Her eyes faded away—those same eyes Lottie once looked into while praying for intercession.

The night Lottie decided to leave the house for good, she'd been up late reading a book when two teenagers kicked over The Blessed Mother, laughing, running back to their remodeled homes up the street. The Blessed Mother lay there, helpless, on the ground. Lottie willed her to get up. Stand up.

But The Blessed Mother didn't move.

Yes, it was time to leave. The next day Lottie was gone. Where would she go? Anywhere but here. The lobby of the hospital, maybe the church's cry room? There were so many places she could tuck in. She settled into a warm spot behind the cheese shop, tried to make friends with the jittery strays.

The bus she rode daily to the mall routed past her once home and she peered from the window to watch the neighbor-man clearing out poison ivy and mayapples from around her house, as many of the weeds the spray could quit, to keep them from crossing the property line and into his space. He cut her hemlocks back, let light in.

Rhododendron burst again on the evening side of the house. Magenta. Stunning colors stirred without all those weeds strangling them out.

Then, without warning, he began filching the perennials. Dug for days. Quartered and transplanted clumps of Stella d'Oros, brown-eyed Susans, tiger lilies, sedum, wild phlox, daisies, hydrangeas, coneflowers, irises, peonies, bleeding hearts. He even dug up the rhododendron and hauled it to *his* evening side. All the faith of Lottie's mother's fingers now grew in another man's yard.

After he was sure his limp transplants rooted in, the neighbor-man let the weeds grow back in Lottie's yard.

A year later, the borough cited her, posting notes on the sun-porch windows dotted by assaults of neighbor boys' BB guns. Code Offenses: High grass. Fire hazard.

The final warning came with a piece in the paper: *Raze the Eyesores!*

At the council meeting, folks claimed her house was the worst on their list, loud enough for her to hear as she sat staring straight ahead. So many whispers. Was it really her in the back row? She wanted to say, Yes, it's me, Lottie Burns. She sensed no one could believe she'd shown up, wondering, *surely she wasn't there to pay those unpaid taxes and stop the Sheriff's sale?* There was no Right of Redemption. They wanted at it. Yes. Wanted a chance to get inside that tight little house, get in that clutter and find what stories, or more, they could underneath all she'd hoarded there, what she'd left behind. Over the years she'd heard everything they'd suspected. Might be silver squirreled in those walls—wasn't her mother's mother a collector? Might be cash nailed underneath those floorboards—didn't her father get a good pension from the mill? Might be bonds basted to the undersides of the mattresses—she'd started buying bonds when her father died in that mill accident, hadn't she?

In that meeting room, she sat there clutching a grocery bag full of clothes and the last of her money, nodding while they carped, jumping a little when the council president hit the gavel.

"They'll get in that house, doped-up punks," one council member warned. All heads bobbed.

Another added, "Old wiring. That house could explode!"

Lottie sniggered when he said that, picturing all the past explosions no one in the neighborhood ever cared to learn about: flung bottles of milk, dandelion wine, corn whiskey. She considered explaining but a man yelled out from the back of the room, voice booming, "Yeah, that damn wiring gotta be nibbled clean through by rats by now. Next thing you know we got ourselves a fire we can't put out."

She laughed a little thinking about how many times her father had threatened, "I'll burn you two to a crisp in this place," nearly touching his cigarette to the gauzy drapes as a warning.

Then a scent caught her. Something new in the meeting room. She raised her chin, sniffed, and found a memory tucked down deep. Her father's Bugler tobacco. He'd told her one evening—a pretty one like this, same lavender sky—how good she was at that task, "How perfect your little fingertips work, Lottie, rolling those cigs." He pursed his lips.

She smiled and sprinkled more tobacco just so, rolled, careful not to rip anything, licked the paper. That was before. She loved before. Before he'd taken her hand, told her to follow him.

But as soon as Lottie allowed that one happy memory to linger, another of her father's pet lines sprung out from a council member's tobacco-packed mouth, brown spittle at the creases of his lips: "Trouble's near. Fat's in the fire." The man closed his pouch of tobacco, hitched up his dungarees, and nodded with certainty just like her father had when he explained her mother would fuel the fire good with all her extra chub.

That's when she laughed and laughed until she couldn't breathe, until her ribs stung. That's when her bag toppled to the floor and people rushed to her, trying to reach their hands inside. She spit, threw her fists, connecting with one person's nose, another's lip. Blood sprayed.

She had withered to eighty-eight feisty pounds, about the same weight she was when she was held down the first time, when her mother went out to deadhead the roses neighbors had once slowed to see. Still, it took four councilmen to get her to the floor and hold her arms.

"Watch she don't hurt herself! Watch you don't hurt her!" a councilwoman yelled. Lottie's mother had said those same words from the hallway when Lottie's father closed the door behind them.

Lottie fought back. She held her legs closed, bit anything that came near her mouth. Then, when she knew she'd had enough, she pounded her head like she'd always done—one loud thump, just enough to bring her mother back in from the garden. This time it wasn't against the maple paneling of her bedroom wall, it was hard, again and again, against the cured concrete council-building floor. She felt her head come open like that muskmelon her father always promised her if she was good, if she just did what he said, just how he told her to do it. A good, sweet-smelling melon with gritty flesh.

Old Lottie died the next day in intensive care, purpled from struggle, strapped down to the last bed she'd have to suffer.

It sold, of course, the house. The bids, embarrassingly low. When the new owner got in, he searched for days but found nothing worth mentioning. No story worth telling in there.

Garage Sale

On my travels today, I came across a telephone pole.
Of venerable age, it was scarred by staples, nails and thumbtacks,
The remnants of a thousand signs for lost pets, guitar lessons and
   garage sales:
The things you need to get rid of quickly or find in a hurry
And some things in between.

Crossing the street, I thought about having a garage sale of my own
Not of household goods;
We hold tighter to our supplies these days, our junk, our bulk
   purchases
We rely on them for solace and survival.

Instead, I want to sell some sins, some old loves and regrets.

But who would want to buy such things?
And what if they offered me a price I couldn't refuse
For the things I wanted to keep?

"My poverty but not my will consents."
I will be like the apothecary
And for forty ducats, instead of poison,
For cold gold or silver,
I will exchange some precious gifts.

First to go would be the things I acquired first:
Memories of my parents, holidays when I was young
The family around a dinner table, everyone alive and healthy
The sound of laughter, the smell of warmth, the feel of wool sweat-
   ers and mirth.

Next would be the high school years:
That great American solipsism, the personal tragedy of puberty
The loss of innocence and the discovery of love mated with passion
Of wild abandon (and here are a few regrets and a few discoveries).

My twenties I will sell cheap, they are not dear to me.
An unvarnished decade, the scene of great promise and great toil
A city life not worth more than a handful of country soil
I will let them go, except for the end, when momentous things
     happened.

Now we come to the best stuff:
Marriage, death and childbirth
The real heart and bone of life

If someone were to come along on the day of my garage sale
A Saturday morning in early spring, perhaps
A brilliant morning, with boundless blue skies
And offer me a million U.S. dollars for my troubles, for my triumphs
Would I be able to resist?

We might haggle a bit about arrangements:
Offshore accounts or investment angles
Interest free loans and collateral,
Grief discounts and joy premiums.

But in the end I might let it all go
Become a different person, enter a new world
To forget again my decisions
And start all over once more.

But one memory I would retain, it's the simplest thing.
You and me by the campfire, alone;

I'm serenading you after you refused me a dance earlier in the
    evening.

You were mad at me but now you're not.
And it dawns on me:
This notion that love and sorrow can coexist,
As night gathers in the crepuscular swamp of twilight.

Chop Wood

For Rebecca

Remember, the ax must be sharp
Otherwise, the work is harder,
But chopping wood is chopping wood,
Not thinking about chopping wood,
Or writing about it,
Or singing it or telling its story.
It is doing work.

And when you do work
The words fall out in a line,
Make a path to follow
And you do.

More wood, more words,
And soon you are down
That path, deep
In that beautiful/terrible place
The work
Has taken you.

Chop wood means chop wood,
But it can and will take you
Anywhere you want
Or don't want
To go.

Insurrection

Today I am both hollow and heavy,
this January sky more ashen than white,
that old elm on the corner leafless, dark.

Even the starlings remain silent, hidden,
make no rustle or ruffle inside morning.
Black dog stays inside,

where the cold won't prickle her arthritis.
Rhododendron curls its leaves
for protection, waits.

Outside, my breath is icy
the air bitter
as the frost of this day,

days gone, days to come,
days insidious
as the ache inside this winter.

Hornets

Braced at the waist, I leaned out the window
of what had become my bedroom & aimed
under the eave a stream of poison that silenced
the winged, furred, wriggling, ferrying hum
& sent after a downbeat the wet, instantaneously
dead colony plummeting to the shingles.
God bless Dow Chemical & give us each day
precise instructions. You didn't watch me

decimate three satellite nests nor prepare
with maniacal rigor the obliteration
of the all-but-undulating northeast corner
of the porch the numbskull landlord
had wrapped in fiberglass siding.
A mourning-dove dusk & how glad
I was we had driven one another far away

from the Cape, Saranac Lake & the secret
crab shack where the butter was frothy
& the ale near-frozen. I waited with yogic
serenity for dying light to tell the last
few hornets to dab their way through
the ill-nailed panels before I drained

the largest can of killer Agway sold
into the corner crack. Oh the hum symphonic!
Twenty square feet of hum! Blissfully soon
the nothing I sought came, once two final
refugees fell black & damp to the grass.

Darkness kept coming, fireflies rose
& the tree frogs could once again
be heard in the busy silence.
I carried the can into the house—

you know how symmetrical I prefer
things to be—& dropped it into the bin
you brought home from K-mart

toward the end, saying "We deserve
nice things" as a wry joke.

At least that's how I took it.

American Meditation, no. 8

For Wasco Temchack Jr., 1925–2012

When I was nineteen, I climbed out of the Moshannon Valley
ran west until I found a place to rest, then slept on the ninth floor,

or drank Yuengling ten floors further up, while my friend fingered
his guitar and sang about watching trains race barges

down the Monongahela. When I was twenty-three, I slept on
top of Mt. Washington. I climbed down then back up,

crossed the Monongahela and Allegheny rivers a thousand times.
In winter, I wore my great-uncle Wasco's army-green, down-lined
    parka.

For years, my only memories of Wasco were the smell of winter-
    green snuff, and
the depths of his cyan eyes. I remembered telling my father that he
    scared me,

then my father tried to explain to a nine-year-old boy what happened
when a nineteen-year-old man dived into a crater like a meteor

alongside men mostly his own age. What happened when he
    inspected his rifle,
peered over the rim of the crater and saw a German, who looked

about his age, and he fell back. How he prayed the German would
    go
the other way before he peered over the rim and saw the German
    again, so he

fell back, and again prayed the German would go the other way. He steadied
his rifle. He fired a .30 caliber bullet through a Nazi's belt buckle.

American men cheered and slapped the killer on the back.
They tried to give him the belt buckle with the hole in it.

Except, I never heard that version until after I turned thirty; my father just always said
Wasco's head got messed up in the war. When I was twenty-three I tasted wintergreen

and felt light as a feather while I prayed over a thousand bridges. When I wore that parka
last winter, I felt a skein become a gaggle in a marsh of greens;

I felt grounded, connected, full.

Tapestry

I trace a finger down your stubbled chin,
the cleft reminds me of the pile of logs out back,
begging to be split. You don't say, but it's a good bet
you share the thought. Work is never far from you—
you with no interest in fickle hobbies.

I left behind a bigger, louder life to live with you
in this forgiving place that is no longer truly wild—
but not yet broken; where untamed shadows
still slink through the hollows and trails zig-zag
through fields of toppled corn stalks.

On our plot, massive oaks, like ancient Amazons
shielding their young, intertwine their gnarled arms
and shelter our nest of twigs. The red oak's broken sprig
pierces my finger as I hang the bird feeder, a drop of my blood
a smear on the oak's open wound. I whisper as I once did
to a childhood friend, "Now we are sisters, obliged one to another."

The stones in the garden, turned up with the plowing
and carried in wheelbarrows to the flower beds,
stand guard between domestic and unruly,
but tame and wild mingle, make love,
create rainbow blossoms so heady and sweet,
the bees swoon. I close my eyes and bend to the stones,
rub a hand over their mossy crowns, the tactile memory of the
damp, fuzzy heads of my own infants beneath my palm.

In winter, walking through the garden's spent flowers,
I sometimes wonder if a day will come when
I snip a thread and unravel from the tapestry that binds me
to this place, leave behind it and you—the shadow that I pass
in the hall each morning—You, who swear you'd disappear
without the light I cast your way.

Kittlelendamwagan: The Earnest One

When I left the Alleghenies for the first time at age 16, it was not my choice. I did not want to leave. My mother consulted with eight uncles and aunts, our minister, two very good friends, and her heart. Six years later, after two years at Wyoming Seminary and four years of undergraduate school at Bard College, when I could have returned, I chose not to, no longer believing I belonged there or anywhere.

Instead, I chose to leave the Alleghenies, the graves of my ancestors, and the West Branch of the Susquehanna River, one of the oldest rivers in the world. *Susquehanna* in Lenni Lenape means *a mile wide and a foot deep*. Originating around 320-340 million years ago, it is older than the mountains through which it flows, created from the Alleghenian orogeny uplift events, when Africa, as part of Gowanda, slammed into the northern part of Euramerica. A noteworthy beginning for a landscape filled with possibility and danger.

I spent time on and in one of the Susquehanna's tributaries, Black Moshannon Creek, which in Lenni Lenape means, *elk river place*. The first time I saw where the Black Moshannon and the Yellow Moshannon merged the water turned dark red for a moment. As a kid, it took my breath away. I went camping there with my family and swam in the cool water. When I was there, I knew I was part of something larger and more mysterious than myself.

Water is receptive, emergent. It has an ancient memory and knows how to follow its path, how to make adjustments, how to merge when needed, and how to deviate and expand. Rivers speak their own language through and across time. I wanted to be the Susquehanna; I yearned to have its attributes.

Rivers have been used by people and animals for many reasons: to stay alive, to set natural boundaries, to keep armies at bay, and to transport people and goods. In a sense, they know how to keep things in and keep things out. I needed to learn that, too.

* * *

Every family has a story. Some families tell their stories over and over again at the dinner table or at bedtime, providing each new generation of listeners with a map describing what hardships were faced, what sacrifices were made, and what wrongs were done to others to gain a foothold. The stories, when they succeed, provide inspiration and warnings, drama and humor, a map with obvious symbols and with mysterious ones.

My family had ones that were written down by a person using a fountain pen; others were clipped from newspapers on the day of the electrocution, or the accident, or the murder. I have turned some of these stories into novels or short stories, poems or essays. When I did, I told the truth of the feeling, the emotion, but not necessarily the facts.

I am an archeologist of time and place, linking stories together to make a map—not to tell others how to travel or where to go—but rather to mark where I have gone and where my ancestors came from and how they arrived in America.

Some stories reveal joy and horror, and pride and shame, and if I am successful, the stories share wisdom and beauty. Other stories become reparation for evil deeds committed and suffered.

For forty years, I have carried around the onionskin paper that my mother typed on when she wrote her version of the past—the pride she felt for her Scotch-Irish-English-German roots and the Great Runaway in Pennsylvania. This branch of our family was indoctrinated into John Wesley's Methodism by the circuit riders, which insisted on balance and moderation in all things, even as John Wesley was having love affairs in Savannah.

I have a hand-written account of my great-great grandmother and great-great-grandfather, their homesteading and their beekeeping along with my father's family tree, drawn by hand in my cousin's perfect penmanship, tracing the Paul line back to their departure from Gravesend, England.

The ancestors vie for my attention, whispering to me in my dreams, *"Tell the story."* I wake in the middle of the night, come down the stairs to my study, and I obey. I am *Kittlelendamwagan*, the Lenni Lenape name for the *Earnest One*. I promised my mother I would turn family facts into stories when she died in 1984. Time is pressing me.

* * *

My childhood was a fairytale, fed by the Grimm Brothers and fueled by images from the Old and New Testament. I journeyed through the German forests and the land of Moses, through Perrault's magic countryside and the windy roads of Nazareth. My mother read folk and fairy tales to me; my grandmother read me the Bible. But the important stories were the ones I heard about dairy farms, electricians, and farmers, about poverty, sacrifice and massacres.

At Snow Shoe Elementary School, I learned about William Penn and living in a commonwealth where decisions were to be made on what was best for sharing natural resources for the common good. I relived the Wyoming Valley massacre. I imagined working in the deep, and often unstable, coal mines of Centre County. I wrote my fourth-grade history paper on the discovery of oil in Titusville.

For my sixth-grade trip, I visited the battlefields of Gettysburg where I thought I heard gunfire. I went to the Hershey factory and practically bathed in chocolate. My parents took me to visit the Liberty Bell with its crack one summer, and then a year later took us to see the great steel mills in Pittsburgh.

At school, we had a map of Pennsylvania on the cover of our tablets. We also had a big map of the state hanging on the wall, beneath the portraits of Lincoln and Washington, that had all the symbols of our state's wealth: forests for timber, mines for coal, derricks for pumping oil.

I was taught implicitly and explicitly that people who lived in the Alleghenies were fighters, workers, homemakers, and patriots, that we knew the truth, told the truth and shared it, and that we could and needed to rely on each other to stay strong.

I grew up Pennsylvania proud.

* * *

Each day was punctuated by chores: cleaning my room, helping feed my grandmother's chickens and collect eggs, stuffing envelopes for my mother's insurance company, practicing piano, raking leaves, and helping to clean the house. I worked as fast as I could so I could sneak off and read.

At the dinner table, my parents talked about schools, their meeting at Mansfield State College, and my father's graduate work at Penn State. I also learned about the tannery in Milesburg that the Shirk side of the family built before the Civil War.

Piano lessons, flute lessons, walks in the woods, and serving at church dinners filled my time. I went to fall festivals and carnivals, worked at the baked goods booth, helped serve at the Lions' dinners and the bazaar. I went on fishing trips with my dad, and never caught anything except tree branches. At night, I read books with a flashlight under my covers. I belonged to my family, and they belonged to me. We all belonged to Snow Shoe, Centre County, Pennsylvania.

Two graveyards provided resting places for those who had come before me—Askey's Cemetery in Moshannon and Advent Cemetery in Yarnell. I visited the cemeteries each spring and each fall to attend to the graves. We packed a picnic lunch to tide us over while we planted geraniums and bulbs.

* * *

My mother told me the story of her ancestors, the Highlanders of Culloden, who chose Prince Charles over George II. She said thousands of them were slaughtered in battle, but some of her bloodline escaped and fled across the Irish Sea. They settled in Ireland's northern counties. Those who lived were declared outlaws by the English; they could be killed at will, their goods seized, and their women molested and raped. There was little food or work in Ireland for the Scots, and so 85,000 of these Scotch-Irish came to Pennsylvania between 1728 and 1776. Their possessions: a Bible, a jug of whiskey, and an ax.

"Our ancestor, Daniel Shirk, arrived in the port of Philadelphia in 1758 where he worked at the docks until he had enough money to travel to Centre County, north and west into the purple and maroon Allegheny

Mountains, part of Northern Appalachia. He settled near Pine Creek, married, and had a son, Jacob, born in 1775.

Rumor traveled south and west about the Wyoming Valley Massacre, and he soon heard rumors about three men being scalped at Pine Creek. Then another rumor reached him that two other men were scalped at the mouth of Bald Eagle Creek.

My mother loved words, so I had to listen; I had to keep up as I shelled peas with her, sitting on the back porch.

"Loyalists to the Crown had joined with members of the Lenni Lenape tribe from as far away as the Wyoming Valley to drive the Yanks who opposed them back south to Philadelphia. Fear of a repetition of the Wyoming Valley Massacre in the summer of 1775 drove Daniel and others back south and east.

All Europeans fled from the mouth of Bald Eagle Creek, and from the North and West Branches of the Susquehanna, stampeding as if they were horses. Some families made rafts, barely held together by dry sticks and string to keep afloat. The women and children rode the water in boats and canoes, while the men walked in single file along the river-banks. By 1782, there were no European settlers living along the West Branch of the Susquehanna."

"None?"

"None."

My mother paused and waited for me to think.

"I'll tell you more tomorrow evening, if you get your homework done before supper."

* * *

That night I dream of moccasin-covered feet, moving almost silently, a whisper, across the ground in the wooded acres behind my house. I know there are no Indians left here.

The next day when I return from school, I wander into the woods carrying a peanut butter and jelly sandwich and my math book. It is my only homework. I plan to sit on the rock pile, eat my snack and do six word problems. But when I arrive, I see a rattlesnake basking. Is it a female waiting to have her baby snakes?

I know to leave her be, and I return to the back porch.

My father's voice echoes in my head: "The timber rattlers live in those woods and what they want is for humans to leave them alone. They make almost no noise unless they are scared, and then they shake their rattles to warn you away."

I know my mother will keep her word, and that after the dinner dishes are done, my mom will tell me more about the Shirks, allowing them to be born again.

* * *

When my mother joins me at the kitchen table, she has a very old piece of paper in one hand and a cup of coffee in the other.

"What's that?" I point to the paper.

"It is the deed to the land on Pine Creek."

"Tell me more."

"Around 1784, Jacob Shirk, Daniel's son, returned to Centre County. He purchased the land he had been living on for a fair price from the Lenni Lenape, as recorded at the Land Office. From then on, he is listed as a resident and taxpayer in the Hamlet of Pine Creek.

"He finished building a house and continued to work the land. Nine years later in 1793, Jacob's son, Joseph Shirk, was born in that house."

I am imagining what the house looked like, how the air smelled, and what sounds were in the background.

"Around 1815 Jacob built a tan-yard in Boggs Township along Bald Eagle Creek, and then rebuilt it some thirty years later at the confluence of Bald Eagle Creek and Spring Creek. He took pride in the quality of the leather he produced. When Joseph Junior took over the business in 1868, the tannery handled 500 hides a year. The company was named Union Leather, and they were proud of their contributions to the Grand Army of the Republic."

"So he is my how many times grandfather?"

"He is your great-great-grandfather. Remember that no matter where you go, your blood goes with you."

I nod.

"You carry this bloodline."

I know, can feel it, and don't say anything. But at night I dream of deep forests, fast running creeks, and wilderness. Men in British uniforms, early Americans in homespun, the Lenni Lenape wearing leather leggings and loincloths.

Soldiers in navy homespun riding south on saddles made at the Union Tannery.

The Lenni Lenape language intact in the names of places: *Pakihmomin*, where the cranberries grow. *Tumanaraming*, where the wolf walks, *Moyamensing*, the place of judgment, *Tulpehocken*, land of the turtles, and the *Susquehanna*, a foot deep and a mile wide.

Reading the Lenni Lenape dictionary, I search for the words that name the work people do: *elogamgussit*, the messenger, *anatschiton*, one who cares, and *kittlelendamwagan*, the earnest one.

I knew then what I know now: it is my job to listen, to learn, and to remember; it is my work to repeat the old stories and to write them down; it is my calling to create new ones.

* * *

At 21, all sixes and sevens with myself, I decided to move to Savannah, Georgia, where I thought I would find my future, could forget my past, and where I could create a present, far away from family judgment. I could fail or I could succeed on my own terms.

I considered myself a writer, but ironically, was ineffective in using words to navigate my life, either saying too little or too much. Confused and overwhelmed by tragedies, beginning with a joint murder-suicide in our family when I was 12, I needed to talk with someone, but shameful things were not talked about in my house or in my town.

Subsequent tragedies followed—ones I thought I should have prevented, but didn't, because, of course, I couldn't. That took me years to figure out.

I was strong and determined in some ways, but not in ways that might have helped me deal with the things I could not control. If life was not going the way I wanted it to, I made change happen; it was how I exerted control. Rashly.

Intensive therapy was needed to address the trauma of my father's accidental and brutal death that had led him to being on a loading dock instead of in his school administrator's office in my local school district. When he'd been reinstated after a two-year court battle, he'd chosen to resign.

* * *

I needed to slow down, to stay put, to have faith. But therapy was not an option in my rural Northern Appalachian town. Snow Shoe was not located in the suburbs of Connecticut or New York or New Jersey.

For people with means and access, therapy was fairly common. Many students at Wyoming Seminary and Bard College had grown up in therapy. Several of my friends talked endlessly about their neuroses and their family patterns, their medications and their Freudian predispositions.

During that time, I was so naïve that I had to find a dictionary and look up *neurotic* after I had an argument with a guy who swore he loved me because I was neurotic. He told me he liked to watch me worry, be nervous, and be sad. That was my sign to stop seeing him.

I began to use the concept of neurosis as a lens for how I looked at the world and the people in it. By the fall of my senior year at Bard, it was clear to me that everyone was neurotic, and it was just a matter of degree. That was the fall one of my aunts was diagnosed with inflammatory cancer at 48.

By driving the six hours home to sit with her at the hospital, I had some delusion that my presence would prevent her death. I went from 115 pounds to 100, and my five-foot, six-inch frame became gaunt.

I decided it was time to go see the psychiatrist who drove to our campus once a week from Albany in his navy-blue Jaguar.

We both smoked cigarettes during the session. I told him the details of my father working on a loading dock after being accused of wrongdoing as a school administrator, that my dad's name had been cleared and he had been reinstated after a court battle, and how after reinstatement, he decided to resign.

I told him my mother used the insurance settlement to send my sister and me to Wyoming Seminary, a Methodist prep school near Wilkes-Barre in order to remove us from the school district where this had happened. I explained that the truck driver at the loading dock where my dad had worked didn't know his gears and went in reverse instead of in drive, and that error had pinned my dad against the wall, breaking his chest, and causing his death later in the ambulance en route to Geisinger. My mother rode with him, and she returned with a broken heart. I described how the truck driver came to our house, literally held up by two men, to apologize to our family.

After an hour, he said, "How did *you* end up at Bard?"

And I realized he had not been listening to me.

"I just told you. Weren't you listening?" I asked.

He looked momentarily uncomfortable, then said, "You need to get over your dad's death, understand that death, even accidental death, is a part of life, stop going to visit your aunt, she isn't going to make it, and make up with your boyfriend. Let him take care of you. Marry him."

I left abruptly and never went back. It took me fourteen years to enter another therapist's door. By then there had been a murder in the family, another aunt had been killed in a car collision, and my daughter had narrowly escaped death.

* * *

Wherever I live or travel, I go in search of water. It is how I feel connected and alive, where I find peace and hope. When I traveled from Savannah to Snow Shoe in 1982, I went first to the bog lands of Black Moshannon State Park and sat for hours thinking about the past.

I listened to the water, seeking clarity about what direction to take from there, wanting to act in measured ways, not rashly.

Sitting on an old picnic table, I stared into the dark water.

People had insulated me from death and dying with silence and euphemisms, but I experienced death at an early age, and in some way had understood and managed it, starting with the coal trucks that passed by my house and ran over our cats.

I knew how to kill, pluck, and prepare chickens for Sunday dinner at what remained of my grandmother's farm. I had watched my cousins drag a deer down from a mountain, gut it, and hang it from a giant pine. But, of course, that was different from losing people I loved.

The state troopers came to my parents' house when I was twelve, rang the doorbell, and announced that my great-uncle had shot his wife, their dogs, and himself. When they showed up at our house, my great-uncle was still alive at Centre County Hospital. I heard my dad say, "It's hard to shoot yourself and get it right."

Angry and hurt because loss is hard, I refused to accept death as part of life. These were people, not cats or chickens. Death comes to everyone, but I had trained myself in magical thinking. I believed if you did all the right things, whatever they were, you could duck death, maybe not forever, of course, but not let it happen to you or those you loved until you and they were well over 70.

After I sat by the water for a while, I got back in my car and drove to my mother's house in Snow Shoe. I had a lot to tell her during this visit before I drove north to Vermont and Bread Loaf's graduate English summer session.

* * *

Being raised on fairy tales and parables was helpful and confusing. I believed that good deeds saved you from death, thought the cure was hyper-vigilance.

I learned about my Grandfather Shope's death when I was ten. My mother sat at her desk, crying. I could hear her sobbing, but she was not producing any tears—after she'd received radiation for skin cancer on her nose, she'd lost her ability to cry because her tear ducts were destroyed.

Hugging her, I asked, "What's wrong, Mommy?"

"I miss my father."

"You haven't told me how he died," I said.

"Sit down."

She went to her hope chest and pulled out a newspaper from 1943 and showed the headline that proclaimed, "Snow Shoe Man

Electrocuted at Clarence Substation." She handed me the paper. I read it. While working in his job as an electrician and consumed by worry about four of his sons and his son-in-law fighting in World War II, he became distracted, and his hat touched a live wire.

I looked up at her.

My mother was quick to add, but if he hadn't died, two of your uncles might well have, since they came home for the funeral. The ship one of them was on was sunk at Pearl Harbor, and another missed being at Normandy.

Implied: Grandpa Frank should have been paying closer attention to his electrical work, which is inherently dangerous. And because he had not been, two of my uncles lived.

There was always a story, a lesson, about someone not paying attention in just the moment when they needed to most. My sweet aunt next door, traveling to work, slid off the road, and before she got out of her car, a truck slid into her and pinned her against a mountain—crushing the life from her. My beloved father, in a moment of picking up garbage at a loading dock, got pushed into a wall and got his chest broken when the delivery man mistakenly went into reverse.

There were other lessons as well. The cautionary tales regarding whom you were going to marry was one of the many talks I received from my mother. It was important, she said, to go through an itemized list on physical and mental health traits. My mom was a storyteller, observant and somewhat judgmental. She used examples from my small town and from within our family to guide us.

My mother had five younger brothers, and she had helped to raise them in her role as oldest child and only girl. She pointed out that one of my uncles had married into a family with mental health issues, and that the aunt's father had severe depression and other issues. He was not a danger to others, but he was a danger to himself, and in his line of work as a barber, he had to take chunks of time off from work and stay away from razors. His grandson, my aunt and uncle's son, had serious mental problems as well. He was diagnosed as schizophrenic and eventually murdered my uncle. There was the proof.

In my mother's lists of warning, a more benign form included her concern about marrying someone with poor vision, balding, fingernail biting, loose morals, tendencies to stutter, poor work ethic, overeating, under eating, alcoholism, and stupidity.

* * *

I know my father was a fisherman because I went fishing with him. I don't know if he was a hunter before he married my mother, but I know he wasn't one after he married her because of an incident in our town where men had gone out hunting, and here is the example of stupidity: someone shot a different aunt's brother thinking he was a deer.

Friends from boarding school lost their minds taking drugs, and a friend from college hanged herself. A roommate after college, who was distracted while driving her VW bug home and crossed over into the oncoming lane, has been hooked up to a machine since 1975.

By the time I was thirty, I was terrified to be alive and had begun to understand how random good and evil were, that we all pretended there was cause and effect, and sometimes, I could even see that there was, but mostly it was just luck—bad or good that damned or saved you.

When a man ran a stop sign two miles from my home in Trumansburg and almost killed my seven-year-old daughter in the back seat of my car, I was pretty much ready to give up on life. All my tricks—finding a good man and a good job, resurrecting an old house, mourning those who had passed, believing in a future where death stayed at bay—had failed if I could not protect my little girl.

Friends came forward, family helped prop me up, I sought help through a psychotherapy called EMDR, and eventually I came back to myself, and I embraced the cliché that every day is a gift. I forced myself to face the past, to write down Truth as I knew it, and to live in each moment for what it was.

* * *

Many of us occupy a liminal space: a position at, or on both sides of a boundary or a threshold—inner and outer, empty and receptive, humble and arrogant—caught in between. Perhaps that is our fate as humans. Sometimes in my life I have been completely present in a positive moment, and when that has happened, I open like a flower in the hot sun of summer. I have also been totally present in tragic moments. In both situations, I see, feel, hear, taste, and smell everything intensely. These moments can last for a brief or an extended period of time, and the imprint is permanent.

At other times, I live anywhere other than the present, projecting myself into past centuries or into a prismatic future.

I have walked a path with confidence and have stumbled over nothing in broad daylight. I forget to consult the map when I am lost; I ignore directions when they don't suit me. I have made choices. Some were excellent, and some were horrible. At my worst, I lacked kindness and discipline, forgot what I knew, and pretended things were one way when they were another. At times, I have faced the truth with boldness and worked an occasional miracle.

A few times I was so hurt that I tore the map up and used it to start fires. Other times, I took pieces of it and covered my wounds. As an author, I have written fiction based on the actuality of my emotions. The stories revealed what I had learned by exploring what I did not understand and turning those experiences toward the light to help myself, and perhaps, to help others.

Sometimes the wind blew hard, and rain and sleet and snow distorted my vision. Sometimes the weather was perfect, the path was clear, and faith and hope flew inside me, a pair of juncos, reminding me I was alive.

I am *Kittlelendamwagan*, the Lenni Lenape name for the Earnest One.

Waiting for the Ball to Drop

We barely kept our eyes open,
but had to see it for ourselves,
the disappearance.

The party was sponsored,
sequined and scored by shooting stars,
heavy with wishes pressed
upon shoulders in every time zone.

Fresh starts require ends.
Regret failed to dissipate, resurrection
never came. The stroke
of midnight settled in furrowed brows.

We did not open champagne,
or buy noise makers, unwilling
to risk the jinx of celebration.

A woman wandered through Times
Square, searching for a mouth to kiss.
I held my breath in prayer,
knowing this might end us all.

Unmoored

Dear Sister,
so much snow fell here last night
the hemlock branches touch the ground.

I took Dad to the window to see
and an airplane like a tiny bird,
in the vast white sky made him ask

When will you be coming home?

* * *

Dear Sister,
So the skin on his sacrum doesn't break down,
I roll him
onto his side and wedge
        the pillow beneath his hip, like you showed me.
Rub the cream on his *scapula, calcaneus, malleolus,*
These words that before language were

so many bony protrusions.

* * *

Dear Sister,
It's important that I name what I can,
leave what I can't, unmoored,

the suffering, the work it takes
to swallow, how he burns more calories chewing
than he gains eating peaches and jelly toast.

We try to think of something easier.

* * *

Dear Sister,
His bed is a skiff.
His feet hang over the gunwale.

He floats between earth and sky,
a soul whose life has just started.
Mom unwraps a cellophane candy.

The sunlight is too loud, too heavy in our arms.

American Meditation, no. 11

Sometimes I think about the Memorial Day

    weekend when I drove back from Virginia,

and my uncle's friend tattooed

    the shape of Pennsylvania into my calf—

because I was homesick—while he told me about

    how his wife found his mother-in-law

swinging among summer dresses.

American Meditation, no. 12

I used to shoot pool with a guy that had a skull tattoo
on the side of his head. And I'd bet it wouldn't surprise you

he had rattlesnakes behind glass in his living room. Or that
his wife was from West Virginia, and I never knew

her real name. But we shared glassy-eyed conversations full of
love as pink as the baby mice in their freezer. So my heart still

shivered when I drove by the house for the first time after
they hung that banner above where we used to shoot the breeze.

Still Dark

From the sugarberry tree,
dove sings her low hello
cardinal his sharp cheer, cheer.

Wren rattles & darts & calls for tea,
while far away, chickadee repeats,
"I'm here, I'm here."

Such exuberance
before the sun
even rises;

such joy
I wish
I knew.

And in this moment,
I do,
I do.

The Bear

A woman dreamed a bear on her back porch
nosing, searching

Somehow, her daughter had captured the bear's cub,
black and bawling

How had she not known?

She opened the door and pushed the baby out,
then locked them in

The mother bear nudged and sniffed her child;
satisfied, the two lumbered toward the woods

The woman thinks her daughter was meant to go with them.
The girl has seen the bears twice in real life.

They will not let her be.
And yesterday she began to bleed.

What can it mean?

No locks can save them from her growing.
The day she pushed the baby out, it began.

She'll look and look to find her, but she's going
wild, a woman, where she thought her child should be.

Transcendence

The road to my mother's home could lead anywhere.
Trees that rest heavy on power lines could be any
trees, and the sky, today void of clouds, could suffocate

any of us. Things are happening this year, bending
on top of strings not made to hold our dead,
like webs I sweep from the corners of my porch.

The news notes those who have left us,
tally-mark reminders of impermanence that we chase
with double bourbons and lethal amounts of blue

light that we cannot soak in fast enough. We dream
about tomorrows that already happened. She starts
a pot of coffee, another leaf surrenders to the ground.

Worth Chewing On: The Log Cabin Years
A Book Review

It could be just a coincidence that, while reading Cindy Ross's *The Log Cabin Years* (Skyhorse Publishing, 2021), I started seeing beavers during my evening hikes along the river near my home.

But I don't think so.

And I'm guessing that Ross wouldn't write off the matter as a mere fluke, either.

Her revelatory story—part memoir, part how-to—leads me to believe that she'd interpret my encounters as serendipitous signs. As nothing less than a stunning synchronicity served up by the natural world to inspire this review of a book about a determined young couple building a living home out of logs that they themselves painstakingly peeled. A book whose 257 pages I consumed with the voracious bliss of a beaver stripping sweet bark.

Like her previous nonfiction books, this latest from Ross affirms the author's deep connection to the natural world. She is profoundly at home outdoors. No plumbing, no central heat, no insulation . . . no problem. In fact, a recurring theme of all her writing is that the less insulated we are from the wild, the better.

In *The Log Cabin Years*, she recalls a deep-rooted yearning: As a girl growing up in suburbia in the 1960s, she dreamed of someday living in a made-from-scratch home of raw trees. A social animal, Ross was not meant to be solitary. She sought a partner whose ingenuity, creativity and productivity matched her own: a mate for life.

Not surprisingly, she met Todd Gladfelter in shared natural habitat. Each was independently hiking the 2,600-mile Pacific Crest Trail in 1981. Forty years later, Gladfelter is her still-sinewy hiking partner and spouse, a chainsaw artist, and father to the couple's two grown children. It's the early years of their four decades together—with a focus on the home they built in the shadow of their beloved Appalachian mountains—that is the wondrous stuff of Ross' latest book.

As the couple learns on the job about techniques and implements—everything from feathering and footers to plumb bobs and picaroons—Ross realizes that mastering softer skills is also vital to their ultimate success.

"It's interesting to observe how Todd and I take turns becoming overwhelmed with the building, losing interest in the work, and falling apart emotionally," Ross writes. "The stronger one has to step up and find the strength to usher both through the hard time, knowing that eventually the tables will turn again, and we will reverse roles."

Revealing the magic of working cooperatively, Ross muses about how ideas become reality most powerfully when all involved appreciate every individual's talents and work harmoniously. Though she characterizes her husband Todd as anything but effusive, she manages to capture him saying, "I really enjoy working with people that I love."

Before I take the beaver analogy any further, let me point out that the team-working rodents epitomize group mind—a balance of communication and purpose possible only without interference from individual egos. Ross is candid about occasions when she and her husband were all too human. "Todd and I fight nearly every day at the building site," she laments, observing, "Fighting feels like poison. . . ."

Their arguing doesn't last nearly as long as the endless scribing and sawing—back-breaking, mind-numbing labor that, not incidentally, leads Ross to a truth worth chewing on: "This building site is our training ground, our school, for life ahead."

Sasquatch

She grew up amid the rubble of urban decay, but one day
she'd had it with the noise, and traffic, the constant babble
of machinery and men, and she hopped a train to the far coast.

The rhythm soothed, the ride opened her airways, and though
she stopped in Denver and L.A. to visit friends, it was the backs
of cities she saw from those rolling windows that made her feel alive.

Back where the rivers join, she packed her final bags, and shot
like a loon for the lakes of Maine, shed clothes like a molting owl
sheds feathers, and once deep in the mountains shed more—

the need for people at all, the need for income, and patience.
With the last of her money, she bought art supplies, made a lean-to
from pine branches and fallen logs, spread a bed of soft needles and
    moss.

The creek became water, and wash, and a place to learn about
    neighbors.
The porcupine she avoided, but found his lost quills anxious for ink,
    the fox
often left hairs from his tail for her brushes. And in this way

she painted a new world, lovely, deliciously lonely, and yet, and yet,
not nearly as lonely as the quick streets of the city, the cell-phoned
    folks
she once called friends. Yes, she grew furry. Yes, she was shy. Yes, yes,

elusive, all of those things. But never the monster you imagined.
Only a woman taking back a life of her own.

What Our Children Know

*Dayton Ohio Youth Orchestra Rehearsal, Pandemic Ritual #17,
10-29-20*

Do not push the elevator buttons, someone will do that for you. Do
    not touch anything,
just say goodbye to your parents and ring the buzzer and someone
    will let you in.

Take the elevator and then take off your shoes. Take your
    instrument out of its case and
carry it under your arm and leave the case in the hallway with your
    shoes.

Carry your stand under the other arm and your music in your
    hands and bring a
pencil and also a water bottle. You must enter alone. You must wear
    a mask and you must

keep it on, unless you need a *mask break* in which case do not ask to
    be excused, just
walk away for a moment and lower your mask. Only go to the
    restroom during

the restroom break, not during the mask break or the water break,
    and keep your mask
on, especially if we begin with Brahms Hungarian Rhapsody #4 in
    C minor, and

especially if we are counting in 2/4 time. Do not raise your hand.
    Do not ask why

you feel breathless. Do you think Brahms, who had all the low and
   heavy tones

of the string bass in his head from the hours of listening to his
   father practice, ever
thought to question his grief? It is yours now. The muted sighs, the
   resonance

of longing reverberating in the music halls of your rib cage. You are
   the echo of
remembrance, the bow pulled across the mournful chambers below
   the strings.

Lilace Mellin Guignard

Thanksgiving Lesson

My son says "Thank you" to the turkey just
before his father brings the cleaver down.
Neither boy nor poultry flinch. It's his first
witness to the deaths that gather 'round
our table. He should know so he can choose.
No ducking the issue with grocery store's
plastic wrapped shelves of disconnected food.
Here—a bucket of heads. We omnivores
are a tormented lot. The spinning plucker
sends feathers spitting out onto the snow.
Yes, there are some dots of red. How should
I explain this slaughter? Was it luck or
plan, how all must eat what breathes or grows?
Gabe says, "Alive it wouldn't taste as good."

Counting Coup

The realization hit me like a boxer's right cross. I was sitting over dinner last week with Donna Rae, chatting about topics I might choose for future magazine articles, when she mentioned I hadn't written anything about my father for a while. I looked at her and experienced a moment of clarity.

"My father lost his willingness to kill," I said, "before he reached the age of 55." She later said my statement sent shivers up her spine. It was so blunt and unexpected.

Until that moment, I had always claimed Powser's poor hunting results were based on two factors: his habit of passing on shots at small game so his three boys would get a chance, and his disinterest in deer hunting, a pastime we boys introduced him to later in his life and which he never took seriously. Powser spent the opening days of rifle buck seasons walking the State Game Lands fire trails socializing with other hunters. Meanwhile, Skip, Billy, and I hunkered down on large mountaintop boulders and kept a vigil all day long for any flash of movement that might be a deer.

Now I know my earlier belief was wrong. For the last 20 years of his life and the last 10 years of his hunting life, Powser stopped shooting because he no longer wanted to kill. This surprises me, since willingness to take the lives of animals is a fact of life for meat eaters and hunters. It's a concept all of us must come to terms with early in our hunting careers.

Here was a man who grew up kicking through the bramble fields of West Middlesex with his father and brother, shooting cottontail rabbits by the dozens for family dinner tables during the Great Depression. Who served as a tank commander for the U.S. Army in Italy during World War II and witnessed loss of life on a scale many of us cannot imagine. Who brought up his own three sons to love hunting and to provide for their families over 25 years of venturing out every autumn small game

Saturday no matter what the weather, no matter what non-hunting concerns might be pressing.

Attitudes can alter in a person over time, and I think I understand. Perhaps you can be a true outdoorsman while walking the woods stalking big game with a camera, or fishing lakes or streams all year but placing every fish back in, like I do with my wild native brook trout. This change has never happened to me—I've killed 12 bucks over the past 20 years—nor did it happen to my younger brother Billy, who shot three deer the last month of his life.

But it did strike my father. I'm sure of that now, and perhaps also my older brother, Skip. He's an aficionado of Pennsylvania reservoirs, where he pilots his old pontoon boat after walleyes and bass. He also practices catch and release. He says he lost interest in hunting 15 years ago because he preferred steelhead fishing in the fall and winter. Also, when his two boys grew up, they preferred fishing over hunting, too. But I wonder.

My friend Gregg told me a few years ago about the old American Indian custom of "counting coup." A warrior could achieve glory by sneaking up on his enemy, touching him with his coup stick, and escaping unharmed. His bravery was then celebrated over great tribal bonfires, and no one had to die. Gregg has been a hunter and meat-eater his whole life, but now that his sons have grown up and moved away and his wife has lost her taste for game food, he's not so inclined to bring home wild game meat for the larder. Lately he says he sometimes draws back his longbow on a deer, sights on the animal's chest, but relaxes the bowstring. Or, he points a 12-gauge at a wild turkey gobbler he has called in on a misty spring morning, aims for a moment, and whispers "bang" under his breath, allowing the bird to slip away. He is counting coup, knowing he has outwitted his prey in the woods but not taken its life.

Perhaps, like my father, he has lost his willingness to kill. Maybe I'll trend in that direction myself one of these days when I'm older and weary of what can happen and what will be. It's a decision not to take lightly, and no one can make it for you.

Eclogue

Outside—O small ones,
To be born!
    —George Oppen

On the sky's gray shawl beyond the windshield
birds scrawl their winter dreams.

Lower, beside the freeway, crows perch
fresh carcasses of lust-drunk bucks.

Hawks freeze halfway between cloud and road.
Heavy brooches, their pale breasts

like my mother and grandmother's cameos
pinned on the brown, otherwise empty, trees.

Quiet farms. Here and there a few dairy cows,
sheep with no shepherd but a donkey.

Else everything waits

like a babe-swollen belly
my doctor takes pictures of
but doesn't touch.

By the time green hands emerge
I'll have a daughter.

Exercise

For Stuart Dischell and his students

Exercise
so
much
you
sweat
poems.

Then poems
will seize
and eat
through so
many yous
like matches

in a match-
book ignited, poems
blazing through you,
words that incise
like knives so
shiny sharp. Whet

them until the whet-
stone breaks and much
of nothing remains. So
you'll know your poems,
then, those shifty spies
who live inside you.

They'll give anything up, you
included. They thirst for sweat,
drink it like wine, exercise
their power until so much
is created, poems birthing poems,
you delirious with insomnia, sow-

ing droplet words to make rain so
the fires might fizzle and you
can sleep. *I want sleep, Poems!*
But I want you too, sweet
fire-eyed devils who know too much—
I sense how great your size.

So you say maybe, my pen sweat-
ing blue yous, my life a burnt match.
The poem played out, for now, exorcised.

Meditation

Of course we will collide with Andromeda. Of course
everyone and everything will die and be reborn.
Your head ends here, but where does your mind end?
Something is lost in the back of it amid dark matter,
expanding what you can't quite put your finger on,
eluding you, slipping under the fence and running off to the fair
with big ideas about flight, bright light, and distraction.
Once you had a dog who tiptoed behind you
—short, slick-black fur, looked like a shadow running beneath the
    moon.
The woods brightly lit, patterns morphed on the forest floor
and she followed close. Next morning you found a gift at the door:
the small clay head of a child that now sits on a cabinet.
My point is this: it's easy to drift with your head in the clouds.
Forget about space. Hold on to January,
when memory of first snow and holidays fade,
when dark-eyed junco and the old blind squirrel compete for seed,
when your feet can no longer stand the idea of themselves without
    socks
and the pups look like prisoners at the window. You see a girl
become a bird and a bird become something
neither of us recognize, an apparition, a far-flung galaxy
advancing like there is no tomorrow.

CONTRIBUTOR BIOS

AB²
AB² is a collaborative writing duo: Kecia Bal, a bestselling author, and Asa Ana, a recognized conceptual artist. Both are rooted in the ancient Appalachians, make their homes in western Pennsylvania, and work at the intersections of community, expression, and nature.

Robert Beveridge
Robert Beveridge (he/him) makes noise (xterminal.bandcamp.com) and writes poetry in Akron, OH. Recent/upcoming appearances in Mawth, The Stray Branch, and Counterclock, among others.

Alex Bischoff
Raised in the Pittsburgh area for much of their life, the author has a keen interest in the local history and can often be found around the local museums and shops. They feel no visit to Pittsburgh is complete without seeing the fountain at the Point.

Sam Bohen
Sam Bohen lives in Erie, Pennsylvania with his two cats. He hopes to live long enough to see the Minnesota Vikings win the Super Bowl.

Anna Marie Donato
Cover artist Anna Marie Donato is an amateur photographer raised in Seminole, PA. An explorer of the forests of Penn's Woods, she is always wondering what she can find, always surprised by her discoveries. Anna Marie loves sharing her work publicly in hopes of stirring a thought or smile.

Don Feigert

Don Feigert has taught at Thiel College, DeVry University, and Daniel Webster College. He has published in Pittsburgh Quarterly, Gray's Sporting Journal, Snowy Egret, Easyriders, Mountain Journal, PA Angler, and Hiram Poetry Review. His two latest books are Trucks Are Better Than Women (humor) and The F-Troop Camp Chronicles (memoir).

Daniel Flatley

Daniel Flatley was born in North Carolina and grew up in Wheeling, W.Va., before enlisting in the Marine Corps in 2004. After leaving the military in 2009, he graduated from Columbia University with a B.A. in English Literature and an M.A. in Journalism with a concentration in business and economics reporting. He has covered state, local and national politics and currently lives near Washington, D.C. with his wife and four-year old daughter. In his spare time, he writes fiction and poetry.

Jane Ann Fuller

Jane Ann Fuller's poetry has appeared in Atticus Review, B O D Y, Grist, JMWW, PMS&G, Pudding Magazine, Rise Up Review, Shenandoah, Still, Sugar House Review, The American Journal of Poetry, The Ekphrastic Review, The MacGuffin, The Pikeville Review; in the anthologies All We Know Of Pleasure, Women of Appalachia Project; and elsewhere.

Angela Gaito-Lagnese

Angela Gaito-Lagnese is the author of the poetry chapbook, Squalling (Main Street Rag, Spring 2021). Her poems have appeared in Nasty Women and Bad Hombres (Lascaux Editions) and other publications. Angela has an MFA in fiction from the University of Pittsburgh and regularly attends Carlow University's Madwomen Poetry Workshops.

Michael Garrigan

Michael Garrigan writes and teaches along the banks of the Susquehanna River in Pennsylvania. He loves exploring the river's many tributaries with a fly rod, hiking the riverlands, and strongly believes that every watershed should have a Poet Laureate. You can find more of his writing at www.mgarrigan.com.

Sandee Gertz

Sandee Gertz is a native of Johnstown, Pennsylvania, currently living in Nashville, Tennessee where she teaches in the English/Creative Writing Department of Cumberland University. She is the author of the poetry collection, The Pattern Maker's Daughter, and has published in numerous literary journals including Gargoyle, Green Mountains Review, The Ledge, and Poet Lore. In 2014, she was featured in *World Literature Today* as one of 16 Working Class Poets. Most recently she has published in The Write Launch where an excerpt from her completed memoir, "Some Girls Have Auras of Bright Colors," was featured in September 2020. She holds an M.F.A. from Wilkes University.

Diane Glancy

Diane Glancy is professor emerita at Macalester College. Currently she teaches in the low-residency MFA program at Carlow University. Her latest book is "Island of the Innocent: a Consideration of the Book of Job." Forthcoming are "A Line of Driftwood: a story of Ada Blackjack" and "The Road is Home: Wandering the Wilderness, Shaping the Spirit." Her other books and awards are on her website, www.dianeglancy.com

Matthew Grolemund

Matthew Grolemund's fiction has appeared in Redivider, The Ampersand Review, Permafrost, Jelly Bucket, Compose, and elsewhere. He is a graduate of the Wichita State University's MFA program and former editor of the program's literary journal, mojo. He currently lives in South Korea, where he is working on his first novel.

Lilace Mellin Guignard

Lilace Mellin Guignard raises kids in Tioga County, PA and has taught creative writing and outdoor recreation leadership at Mansfield University. She is the author of the adventure memoir, When Everything

Beyond the Walls Is Wild: Being a Woman Outdoors in America, and the chapbook, Young at the Time of Letting Go.

Richard Hague

Richard Hague is a native of Steubenville, Ohio and author or editor of 20 volumes, including Riparian: Poetry, Short Prose, and Photographs Inspired by the Ohio River, edited with Sherry Cook Stanforth (Dos Madres Press, 2019). He continues as an Artist-in-Residence at Thomas Moore University in northern Kentucky.

Pauletta Hansel

Pauletta Hansel's eighth poetry collection is Friend, epistolary poems written in the early days of the pandemic; her writing has been in Oxford American, Rattle, Northern Appalachian Review, Pine Mountain Sand & Gravel, Still: The Journal, and New Verse News, among others. Pauletta was Cincinnati's first Poet Laureate (2016-2018). https://paulettahansel. wordpress.com/.

Lisa Harris

Lisa Harris, MFA, is from the Allegheny Mountains of Central Pennsylvania. Her publications include novels: 'Geechee Girls, Allegheny Dream, and The Raven's Tale, (Ravenna Press) and poetry, Traveling Through Glass, Dwelling Space, (Cayuga Lake Books) and Broken Open, (Wasteland Press.)

Kirk Judd

Kirk Judd has lived, worked, fished trout, and wandered around in West Virginia all of his life. Kirk was a member of the Appalachian Literary League, a founding member and former president of West Virginia Writers, Inc., and is a founding member and creative writing instructor for Allegheny Echoes, Inc.

Stephanie Kendrick

Stephanie is the author of Places We Feel Warm, set to be released this February by Main Street Rag. She has appeared in Sheila-Na-Gig, Women of Appalachia Project's Women Speak, Ghost City Review, Northern Appalachia Review, and elsewhere. You can also find her on the Poetry Spoken Here podcast.

Cathy Cultice Lentes

Cathy Cultice Lentes lives in southeast Ohio. She is the author of Getting the Mail (Finishing Line Press, 2016), and she holds an MFA in Writing from the Solstice Program of Pine Manor College. Her poetry and essays appear in various literary journals and anthologies.

Jimmy Long

Jimmy Long's poems have appeared in Appalachian Review, Appalachian Journal, Still: The Journal, and Kestrel, among other regional publications. His work also is forthcoming in Presence: A Journal of Catholic Poetry. A native of Buckhannon, West Virginia, Long works and lives in Charleston with his family of five.

Paula Makris

Paula Makris lives in Wheeling, WV and is an associate professor of English at Wheeling University, where she teaches literature and creative writing.

Erica Manto-Paulson

Erica Manto Paulson's poems have appeared most recently in Thimble Literary Magazine, The Adanna Literary Journal, Vol.1 of the Northern Appalachia Review, and The Dayton Anthology, among others. Her first chapbook is forthcoming from Finishing Line Press. When not writing, she crafts poetry in her head while driving between home births as a midwife assistant, and sometimes she remembers to jot them down.

Jolene McIlwain

Jolene McIlwain's work appears online at Cincinnati Review, Prairie Schooner, Prime Number, Atticus Review, Litro, New Orleans Review, and elsewhere. She was named finalist for Glimmer Train's New Writers and VSF contests. Her fiction has been nominated for Pushcarts, Best of the Net, and was included in Best Small Fictions 2019.

annie mcwilliams

Born in Martins Ferry and raised in Columbus, annie mcwilliams is a daughter of the American Revolution. Retired from state prison & addictions nursing, she has worked election polls for 14 years, is a member of Ohio Poetry Association and Columbus Poetry Salon and has been published in anthologies & zines.

Martha Gallagher Michael

Martha Gallagher Michael is a professor of education at Capital University, and a professional artist in metalsmithing, oils, acrylics, printmaking, and collage. She exhibits her work locally and regionally and has published her poetry and art (as 2 covers) with Pudding Magazine and published both art and poetry at Steinbecknow.com.

Jim Minick

Jim Minick is the author of five books, the most recent, *Fire Is Your Water*, a novel. *The Blueberry Years*, his memoir, won the Best Nonfiction Book of the Year from Southern Independent Booksellers Association. His work has appeared in many publications including The New York Times, Poets & Writers, Tampa Review, Shenandoah, Orion, Oxford American, and The Sun.

Nichola Moretti

Nichola Moretti currently lives in Pittsburgh, but grew up in Meigs County, Ohio. She is a freelance writer and an adjunct professor at Robert Morris University and the Community College of Allegheny County.

Ben Moyer

Ben Moyer's writing on nature, outdoors, and conservation appears in numerous regional and national publications. He is a recipient of the Outdoor Writers Association of America's Excellence in Craft Award for lifetime body of work. Moyer lives with his wife Kathy in rural Farmington, Fayette County, Pennsylvania.

Deni Naffziger

Deni was raised in Ohio's Appalachian Steel Valley but has called Athens County, Ohio, home for over 30 years. Deni's most recent book, Desire to Stay, was published by Stockport Flats Press in 2014, and their poems have appeared in The New Ohio Review, Pine Mountain Sand & Gravel, Women of Appalachia Project, Spoon River, Pikeville Review and others.

Karen Whittington Nelson

Karen Whittington Nelson lives in rural Southeast Ohio. She writes poetry and fiction and presents her work with the Women of Appalachia Project (WOAP). Her most recent poetry appears in Gyroscope Review, Winter, 2021, the anthology, "Women Speak", Volume 6, as well as the forthcoming, "Anthology of Appalachian Writers", Dorothy Allison, Volume 13.

Valerie Nieman

A native of western New York, Valerie Nieman was a journalist and farmer in West Virginia. Her fourth novel, To the Bones, came out in 2019 from West Virginia University Press. Her poetry has appeared in three collections, several anthologies, and journals from The Georgia Review to The Galway Review.

Edwina Pendarvis

Edwina Pendarvis' work appears in Appalachian Journal and Journal of Appalachian Studies and other regional and national publications. Her most recent poetry collection, Ghost Dance Poems, was published by Blair Mountain Press. Her writing reflects her commitment to the Appalachian region and its egalitarian spirit.

Jaclyn J. Reed

Jaclyn J. Reed received her MFA in Fiction Writing from Carlow University/Trinity College, Dublin and her BA in English from the University of Pittsburgh. Her work has appeared in Prime Number Magazine, The Write Launch, and Open Minds Quarterly, among others.

John Repp

John Repp grew up along the Blackwater Branch of the Maurice River in southern New Jersey and has lived for many years in Erie, Pennsylvania. Broadstone Books will soon publish a volume of selected and new poems entitled The Soul of Rock & Roll: Poems Acoustic, Electric & Remixed, 1980-2020.

Alice I. Reynolds

Alice I. Reynolds is a writer with an educational background in rhetoric and composition. She belongs to a local writer's group and has contributed work to the group's online anthologies, including The Gift and Love Will Always Find You. These anthologies may be viewed online at: https://dgaskill.wixsite.com/sowriters

Barbara Sabol

Barbara Sabol's fourth poetry collection, Imagine a Town, was published in 2020 by Sheila-Na-Gig Editions. Her work has appeared most recently in Evening Street Review, One Art, Literary Accents, and Modern Haiku. Barbara's awards include an Individual Excellence Award from the Ohio Arts Council. She lives in Akron, OH.

Linda Schifino

Linda Schifino is Professor Emerita of Communication at Carlow University, where she is also an MFA candidate in Creative Nonfiction. Linda is currently writing a memoir in essays describing growing up in an

Italian-American enclave in Pittsburgh in the 1950's. She has had essays published in DoveTales Literary Journal, Adelaide Magazine, and Voices from the Attic Vol XXIV and XXV.

Jacob Strautmann

Jacob Strautmann's The Land of the Dead Is Open for Business is available from Four Way Books. Awarded a 2018 Massachusetts Poetry Fellowship by the Massachusetts Cultural Council, Jacob Strautmann's poems have appeared in Salamander Magazine, The Boston Globe, The Appalachian Journal, and Southern Humanities Review. www.jacobstrautmann.com

Thomas E. Strunk

Thomas E. Strunk teaches Classics in Cincinnati where he now lives. He grew up in Minisink Hills, Pennsylvania on the Delaware River. He is the author of History after Liberty and has written on Dr. King as a reader of the classics, Latin poetry, and the music of Bob Dylan.

Jordan Tyler Temchack

Jordan Tyler Temchack is a poet, folksinger, and illustrator. He lives with his partner and dogs in Central Pennsylvania, where they garden and wander around the Allegheny Mountains. His work can be found at Prime Number Magazine, Red Flag Poetry, Passengers Journal, or his website: https://jordantylertemchack.wordpress.com.

Kimberly BMW Wade

Kimberly BMW Wade lives in Ohio with her husband and two cats. Most recently, she published in the Coffin Bell journal of dark literature, Eye to the Telescope literary magazine, Tequila Kraken: An AWFUL Publication, and received honorable mention for the 2019 SFPA Contest. http://kimberly-bmw-wade.weebly.com

Caroline Wermuth

As outreach coordinator for the Pennsylvania Center for the Book in the Penn State University Libraries, Caroline Wermuth coordinates the

Public Poetry Project, Lee Bennett Hopkins Award for Children's Poetry, and Lynd Ward Prize for Graphic Novel. Her poems have appeared in Northern Appalachia Review, Frogpond, and World Haiku Review.

Sherrell Runnion Wigal

Sherrell Runnion Wigal is a West Virginia poet. Her poetry appears in many publications throughout the country, including, Streetlight Magazine, Pine Mountain Sand & Gravel, Women of Appalachia Speak and Sheila-Na-Gig. Much of Sherrell's poetry reflects her love, appreciation and connection to nature, people, and her cultural heritage.

Colin Williams

Colin Williams (he/him) grew up in Northeast Ohio and holds an MFA from the University of Florida. He lives in Pittsburgh, where he writes, embroiders, and works in arts education. His writing has previously appeared in Hobart and Rain Taxi Review of Books.

Alexandra MacKenzie Wilson

Alexandra MacKenzie Wilson currently works as a Customer Success Advocate, but her first love is writing. She has a master's degree in Industrial Organizational Psychology and earned her undergraduate degree from Clarion University, majoring in Mass Media Arts, Journalism, and Communication Skills with a minor in creative writing. She enjoys writing, traveling, and creating new recipes.

Maryalice Yakutchik

Maryalice Yakutchik is a longtime writer of nonfiction for newspapers, magazines, and websites, as well as the author of several books. She has been a regular contributor of book reviews to the Baltimore Sun, among other media outlets.

www.ingramcontent.com/pod-product-compliance
Lightning Source LLC
Chambersburg PA
CBHW032213030726
47494CB00020B/1002